CALIFORNIA ACADEMY OF SCIENCES

25 March 2009
Happy Birthday
my
Sweet Son

All my love
Mom

CHRONICLE BOOKS
SAN FRANCISCO

CALIFORNIA ACADEMY OF SCIENCES

ARCHITECTURE IN HARMONY WITH NATURE

By SUSAN WELS
Preface by GREGORY C. FARRINGTON
Foreword by RENZO PIANO
Introduction by JOHN E. MCCOSKER

Design by NOON

Library of Congress Cataloging-in-Publication Data available

ISBN: 978-0-8118-6514-2

Manufactured in the United States of America.

The interior pages are printed on Forest Stewardship Council certified paper containing 30% recycled content.

10 9 8 7 6 5 4 3 2 1

Chronicle Books LLC
680 Second Street
San Francisco, California 94107

www.chroniclebooks.com

CONTENTS

Exploring the world is a process of wonder and joy, and science lets us explain and understand it. Today, however, standing for science and its pivotal place in the post-Enlightenment world can be unpopular. In the seventeenth century, Galileo was attacked for espousing naturalistic instead of supernatural explanations for the paths of the planets. In our own time, the conflict over creationism and evolution has revived the clash between supernatural and rational understandings of life on Earth.

The California Academy of Sciences stands for scientific exploration and explanation as the best way to understand the world. Scientific discovery is one of the most exhilarating human experiences—finding a new species, for example, and discovering how it relates to others and how it evolved. Sharing that knowledge and amazement at life's diversity is what the Academy of Sciences is all about.

This institution is also deeply engaged in two of the greatest, most provocative questions of our time: What is life—how did it get here and evolve? And how can we protect and sustain life so it—and we—survive? Today we are on the verge of harnessing our knowledge of DNA to tinker with life itself. We are also, for the first time, acknowledging worldwide that the sustainability of life is a serious question. In years to come, these issues will drive fundamental decisions in our society and the world at large, and they will challenge many systems of belief. The Academy's research can play a role in clarifying these global issues, and our resources can help explore and explain their profound importance.

At the same time that its central concerns are claiming world attention, the California Academy of Sciences has had the unique opportunity to reinvent itself—not just physically but in every way. Our elegant new building is itself an exhibit of the creativity that evolution has made possible. But what really matters is what goes on inside—the programs, research, and commitment to understanding life on Earth and how to sustain it.

As we go forward, the California Academy of Sciences will be not only the best in the West but also one of the best in the world at engaging and inspiring people to care about the rich diversity of life and its survival. Our research has long had a global reach, and the world is watching what we do because of the boldness of the transformation we've undertaken. We are committed to science, to exploring and explaining the natural world, and to making it fun. Joy and wonder, after all, open the mind—and the heart—to a reverence for life on this planet and the will to sustain it.

FOREWORD *by Renzo Piano*

It has been a great adventure.

This is the only thing that I could express in words: to build the new building of the California Academy of Sciences in San Francisco's Golden Gate Park has been a great adventure.

As an architect, I hope I have been able to express all the rest through the building itself: the poet expresses himself through his poems, the musician through his music, the writer through his words, and the architect through his buildings.

It has been a great adventure also because it has been extraordinary to work with scientists on their home ground.

To explore forests, to plunge into deep sea waters, to peer at nature and discover its secrets: all these things inevitably inspire a building that wants to be an exploration ground itself.

This is why the roof became a living surface with native California plants and wildflowers that grow and multiply, and the piazza is covered by a subtle spiderweb made of steel cables and thousands of small photovoltaic cells that capture solar energy.

This building has the ambition to direct the architect's attention toward a new language, inspired more by nature and by the energy contained within it.

Our century opens with an unexpected discovery: the Earth is fragile.

Therefore the architecture should learn to breathe with the Earth's rhythm.

Welcome into the new world of the California Academy of Sciences.

A wild scene, complete with stuffed mastodon, greeted visitors to the California Academy of Sciences' Market Street headquarters. The 1906 earthquake and subsequent fire destroyed the ornate building, along with most of the artifacts it housed.

A BRIEF HISTORY OF THE WEST'S OLDEST SCIENTIFIC INSTITUTION

By John E. McCosker

For more than 155 years, the California Academy of Sciences has been exploring and explaining the natural history of the American West and beyond and, by its actions, protecting the splendor and resources of our planet.

It all began in the town of Yerba Buena, a sleepy village of 375 residents prior to the California gold rush of 1849. By 1853, the population had grown to fifty thousand, and the city had become the largest metropolis along the Pacific Coast. With the discovery of gold came educated men who realized that other natural resources— plants, animals, and minerals—abounded. Many of these resources were unfamiliar to them, and they were eager to understand and classify their discoveries. To that end, a group of seven men met at 129 Montgomery Street on April 4, 1853, to discuss the organization of a society for the promotion of science. It was to be called the California Academy of Natural Sciences (renamed the California Academy of Sciences in 1868), and it became the first scientific organization in the western United States—older than the Pony Express and the *Origin of Species*. Its founders realized:

> We have on this coast a virgin soil with new characteristics and attributes, which have not been subjected to a critical scientific examination. Sufficient, however, meets the eye of the naturalist to assure him that this is a field of richer promise in the department of natural history in its variety than has previously been discovered.

These were men of action, and perhaps those were simpler times. They wrote a constitution, appointed geologist and entrepreneur Andrew Randall as president, and on June 27, the Academy became legally incorporated. The constitution read, "Scientific gentlemen may be received as resident members," and within a month about forty had been enrolled. The new Academy became the first such institution in the world to include the fairer sex. On August 1, 1853, it was "resolved, as the sense of this society, that we highly approve of the aid of females in every department of natural history, and that we earnestly invite their cooperation." That extraordinary action was followed some years later by the appointment in 1883 of botanist Mary Katharine Layne Curran Brandagee as the Academy's first paid curator; in the following year, Rosa Smith Eigenmann became the first female curator of ichthyology of any museum. Other barriers were broken, including the election in 1887 of the Academy's first Hispanic board member, Eusebius J. Molera, who later became the board's president.

After incorporation, the members began to accumulate a library and collection of specimens at 622 Clay Street, the first science museum in the West. The proceedings of each meeting were published in the *Pacific*, a Congregationalist newspaper, and included a series of observations and species descriptions that are still valid today. The orderly sequence of meetings and presentations was not interrupted even by the murder of President Randall on July 24, 1856, by Joseph Hetherington, a gambler to whom Randall was indebted. The minutes of the subsequent meeting reported on descriptions of new coniferous trees and that Academy members had attended Randall's funeral (and, although not recorded, Hetherington's hanging by the Vigilance Committee).

The Academy's constitution also allowed for corresponding and honorary members, a list that would ultimately include such scientific luminaries as Louis Agassiz, Prince Charles Lucien Bonaparte, Charles Darwin, Sir William Hooker, Josiah Dwight Whitney (head of California's Geological Survey, for whom the state's highest peak is named, and eventually a president of the Academy), Major John Wesley Powell (who explored the Grand Canyon), and Stanford president David Starr Jordan. Another early member was John Muir, who in 1892 founded the Sierra Club at the Academy. (The records report that Muir was eventually removed from the membership rolls for nonpayment of dues.) Perhaps the first professional naturalist to join the Academy was Hans Hermann Behr, who shared his linguistic talents with other members in naming new species. He despised "scientific humbugs" and "professional quacks" and took great joy in naming a particularly obnoxious louse after one of his detractors. Also among the most significant early members was James Blake, a Briton who arrived in 1849 and became a professor of midwifery and diseases of women and children at Toland Medical College of San Francisco. Thanks to Blake's innovative approach to malolactic fermentation, California became the producer of fine wines it is today.

Academy members searched and discovered in earnest amid the bountiful biodiversity of the Far West and the Pacific Coast. During 1898 and 1899, Academy scientists participated in the Harriman Expedition to Alaska, followed in 1903 by a major expedition to the Islas Revillagigedo, off Mexico. The Academy's discoveries and its scientific renown attracted the interest of railroad barons Leland Stanford and Charles Crocker. With their support, the Academy's museum relocated in 1874 to the First Congregational Church of San Francisco, at the corner of California Street and Grant Avenue. There it remained until 1890, when San Francisco's "miserly millionaire," James Lick, deeded a large property at 833 Market Street to the Academy to build "one of the most magnificent temples of science on the face of the globe." Two elaborate buildings were constructed in 1891. The museum in the rear was on a par with the great museums of the time, with life-size restorations of dinosaurs and a mammoth and skeletons of an African elephant and an Irish elk. The Academy was a popular and thriving institution until it ceased to exist at 5:12 on the morning of April 18, 1906.

The great San Francisco earthquake and fire destroyed most of the Academy's collections. All would have been lost were it not for the courageous actions of Alice Eastwood, the Academy's curator of botany, Academy director Leverett Mills Loomis, and others who rescued nearly a thousand botanical specimens, records, and other materials. Meanwhile, as San Francisco shook and burned, the Academy's namesake schooner was returning from a monumental two-year voyage of exploration and collection to the Galápagos Islands. She had left San Francisco on June 28, 1905, with a professional collector named Rollo Beck and seven young scientists on board and returned on November 29, 1906, with the most comprehensive collection of plants and animals ever assembled at Galápagos. The hardy but exhausted crew threw their old clothes overboard "so the Board of Health will not hold us up." Their discoveries would constitute the nucleus of the Academy's new collections.

An amendment to the city charter passed by the voters in 1910 authorized the Academy to relocate to Golden Gate Park. Using donations and insurance funds, the Academy was rebuilt and occupied in 1914. The new building was immediately condemned, because beach sand rather than clean sand had been used in its construction; it reopened in 1916, after renovations.

The first public exhibits at the new museum were the North American Halls of Mammals and later of Birds. They were groundbreaking in that they displayed large habitat groups of animals in a new manner, now known as "dioramas." Each diorama was a group effort, involving a taxidermist (usually the specimen collector), a botanist, a geologist, and an artist. The mural backdrops, many by Charles Bradford Hudson, were renowned as the most realistic ever painted. The halls were like natural history cathedrals, paneled with dark wood, with the dioramas illuminated by skylights.

STEINHART AQUARIUM n 1914, Barton Warren Evermann, a protégé of David Starr Jordan, America's leading ichthyologist and the president of Stanford University, arrived in San Francisco to direct the California Academy of Sciences. A highly respected scientist, Evermann was a true believer in the importance of museums, as well as a fine fund-raiser. In 1920 he wrote in the *American Angler*, "Men and women of wealth are more and more coming to realize that there is no more satisfactory way of disposing of their wealth than by giving it to scientific and educational institutions to aid in the increase of knowledge and its diffusion among men." Armed with that ethic and a love of fish, Evermann soon learned of Ignatz Steinhart's interest in creating an aquarium. Steinhart assured Evermann of a substantial gift if the new aquarium could be located in Golden Gate Park, under the control of the Academy of Sciences, with its ongoing maintenance paid for by the city. In his will, Steinhart ultimately provided the funds for an aquarium "second to none in the world," in honor of his brother Sigmund.

Influential San Franciscans such as M. H. de Young and John McLaren, the "father" and superintendent of Golden Gate Park, were enthusiastic. Prior to the 1906 earthquake, designer Willis Polk had spoken for many when he declared that the city was "an architectural nightmare conceived in a reign of terror . . . by artistic anarchists." He and his colleagues had welcomed the temblor and with Crocker began a campaign to improve the haphazard quality of San Francisco's visage.

Lewis Parsons Hobart was selected as the aquarium's architect. He had designed the Academy buildings in Golden Gate Park, as well as dozens of downtown commercial buildings, including the Bohemian Club, Mills Tower, University Hospital, and Grace Cathedral. But the new Steinhart, with its grand facade, columns, sunken entry pools, and interior swamp, as well as the appearance and function of its innumerable aquarium displays, would receive the greatest acclaim. At its completion, the Steinhart would have more cubic feet of water than any of the nation's other public aquariums.

Construction began on April 1, 1922, and within a year was nearly completed. The total cost was $303,000 (the 2008 equivalent would be approximately $4 million), slightly under budget. The first inhabitant was a yearling harbor seal named Pete. Other animals came from a variety of sources, including the Matson Navigation Company, whose steamships regularly brought specimens from Hawaii, Pago Pago, and Papeete.

Robert L. Ripley, the creator of *Believe It or Not!*, took regular pleasure in announcing that the Steinhart Aquarium was overseen by a seal. Alvin Seale, the first superintendent of the Steinhart, regularly enjoyed the pun, but he was much more than the overseer of fishes. He was a colorful adventurer, explorer, naturalist, and soldier of fortune who could have been the archetypal hero of *Raiders of the Lost Ark*. Born in Indiana in 1871, Seale had listened intently when David Starr Jordan spoke at his high school graduation. Jordan advised the students to "go

where the masters taught," so Seale rode his bicycle across the country to enroll at Stanford. Seale designed, oversaw the construction of, and supervised the aquarium's exhibits with flair and excitement for twenty years. His South Pacific expeditions in search of creatures and cannibals drew sold-out audiences to his lectures upon his returns.

The Steinhart Aquarium attracted more than 2,500 visitors on September 29, 1923, its opening day, and 232,947 in its first month; by December the monthly total exceeded 350,000. The November 4 *Oakland Tribune* proclaimed that "no benefaction that San Francisco ever enjoyed gained such instant popularity as the Steinhart Aquarium. It is thronged through weekdays, and on Sundays there is a crush."

The Steinhart became even more popular during the Depression and World War II. It had become world famous for its displays, and by its twenty-fifth anniversary had been visited by twenty-two million people—more than the population of the eleven western states at the time. Among the visitors that year were Rita Hayworth and Orson Welles, who appeared in the aquarium's swamp and among the darkened displays during filming of the 1948 romantic film noir *The Lady from Shanghai*.

EARL HERALD Alvin Seale was succeeded by Earl S. Herald, whose name to generations of mid-twentieth-century Academy visitors became symbolic of the Academy itself. Herald's overarching persona became so familiar to Bay Area residents that the aquarium outshined the rest of the Academy, and the entire institution became known to most as "the Steinhart," with Earl its invincible captain.

The collections grew under Herald. Reptile and amphibian displays were expanded from a single boa constrictor to one of the world's largest and most diverse displays. Herald's secretary, Phyllis Ensrud, described his collection philosophy: "There are two schools of thought on displaying animals in an aquarium: The 'Tiffany' approach considers the epitome to be a single jewel or at the very most, a small collection of gems in one tank. On the other hand, the 'Barbara Hutton' style typifies the old-time, five-and-dime stores' jumbled windows." The Steinhart followed Barbara. The fishes became so abundant, aquarist Lloyd Gomez told me, that the staff lived by Herald's motto, "I don't want to see any water!"

It was through television that Herald and "the Aquarium" became household words not just in the Bay Area, but around the world. Herald produced and hosted *Science in Action,* a weekly evening program, for fourteen years (1952 to 1966). It began in the days of live television. Although camera shy at first, Herald quickly overcame that encumbrance and learned to ad-lib with ease, making his guests and audience comfortable. Each program ended with Herald announcing, "Now don't go away. I'll be back with the 'Animal of the Week.'" He'd return to show a frightened bandicoot biting its handler or a possum peeing on his own white lab coat. Without missing a beat, Herald would remark, "If your picture is a bit out of focus, it's because the cameraman just turned green and fainted." The program received dozens of local, national, and international awards, and were it not for its exorbitant production costs in the mid-1960s, it probably would have continued. The Academy still owns the brand name *Science in Action,* which continues as a radio show hosted by Jerry Kay, broadcast every weekday since 1983 on radio science spots in the Bay Area and beyond.

AFRICAN HALL African animals have long played a key role in the Academy's history. African Hall, which opened in 1936, proudly displayed the plants and animals of sub-Saharan Africa at a time when most visitors knew them only from black-and-white photos in *National Geographic*, movie newsreels, *Tarzan,* and *King Kong*. In 1983, exhibit designer Kevin O'Farrell broke with museum tradition when he and the exhibits staff removed the glass from the large water-hole display at the east end of the hall and allowed visitors to experience the changing sounds of the different water-hole inhabitants as the display underwent a day-to-night transition every fifteen minutes. While exhibit legends were regularly modernized as new techniques and new information became available, one thing never changed—the serene mountain gorilla standing sentry before the restrooms.

MORRISON PLANETARIUM Director Robert Cunningham Miller (1938 to 1963) was a trained marine biologist who studied marine invertebrates and wrote papers and books while shepherding the Academy through the end of the Depression, the war years, and the birth of the Morrison Planetarium, the Morrison Auditorium, and Astronomy Hall. The planetarium opened in 1952 with funds donated in memory of Alexander Frances Morrison from the estate of May Treat Morrison. The key to its success was its remarkable star projector, made possible by the Rosenberg Foundation.

Credit for the planetarium was largely due to the ingenuity of G Dallas "Doc" Hanna, the Academy's diatomist. In 1942, Doc had established an optical shop in the museum to grind and polish lenses, prisms, telescopes, and even periscopes used by the U.S. Navy's Pacific Fleet. The shop was staffed by amateur telescope makers and, at the end of his workday, by Director Miller. Prior to World War II, a company called Zeiss had built all large planetarium projectors. But by 1948, Zeiss, which was located in East Germany, had become inaccessible, so the Academy took advantage of its sophisticated optical shop and designed and built its own.

Doc and Albert S. "Jimmy" Getten, the Academy's most distinguished inventor and instrument maker, used war surplus materials to create the unique projector. Rather than being shaped like a large dumbbell, with planetary spheres at each end, theirs centered the mass to provide balance and stability. Rather than drilling tiny holes in the spheres through which "starlight" would pass, they placed grains of Carborundum—silicon carbide crystals—upon a glass plate precisely in the position of actual constellations, coated the plate with vaporized aluminum, then brushed off the grains. Unlike the "stars" of drilled-hole projectors, the stars from these irregularly shaped glass holes twinkled.

The projector would be state-of-the-art for much of the next fifty-six years. Nothing except the clear night sky could compete with the Morrison Planetarium. It ran seasonal shows during the day and evening and in 1958 pioneered the planetarium light-and-music experience with a show called Vortex. As the years passed, Vortex evolved through a variety of classical, jazz, and New Age agendas until 1974, when it became a highly successful (and income-producing) multicolored laser-light show known as Laserium, featuring the near-deafening sounds of Pink Floyd and the culture of the Haight-Ashbury neighborhood. The success of such an acid-rock experience was particularly ironic, given that the planetarium's director was retired naval captain Robert D. Risser, a most conservative gentleman who thought "grass" was what he mowed every Saturday.

HOHFELD *and* BOTANY HALLS Before entering the planetarium, visitors observed the 240-pound Foucault pendulum in the adjoining Hohfeld Hall of Space Sciences, suspended from the thirty-foot-high ceiling and swinging slowly back and forth over an ornate compass rose, knocking over a wooden peg every sixteen minutes as the Earth rotated on its axis. Smaller Foucault pendulums were made by the Academy staff and sold to museums around the world.

Hohfeld Hall, created with funds donated by Lillian Devendorf Hohfeld, also offered a series of displays about astronomy. One exhibit allowed visitors to step on a scale and discover their weight on Earth, the Moon, or Mars. The first "Shake Table" provided nervous, giggling young-sters with a simulated earthquake experience. It became so popular that it was transformed into the Earthquake Theater in Lovell White Hall, complete with a massive temblor activator.

Botany Hall was named in honor of Alice Eastwood, curator of botany from 1892 until her retirement in 1949, at age ninety. Opened in 1959, the hall possessed numerous displays, ranging from mushrooms and ferns to exquisite flowering plants, and was the home of a massive crosscut Sequoia slice taken from a 1,710-year-old tree. Rings from that massive slab were correlated with events in human history, provid-ing visitors with an opportunity to learn what this tree was doing when the Magna Carta was signed and when our nation was founded.

MIDCENTURY *at the* ACADEMY Academy attendance grew during the halcyon days of the 1950s. There was no entrance fee prior to 1969, but counters installed at the doors accounted, conservatively, for nearly two million visitors a year.

As the Steinhart Aquarium matured, its fame grew and its blemishes became more apparent. The continuous year-round operation, the pump-ing and spilling of saltwater, and the creation

of a steamy indoor tropical environment took their toll. On June 3, 1958, San Francisco voters approved Proposition B, to renovate the Aquarium, by a comfortable margin. In 1963, the year the aquarium reopened, 3.5 million visitors came through the doors, the highest number ever recorded for any San Francisco attraction. The swamp was modified and became a large reptile display, and the entrances to the aquarium became long, tank-lined corridors. The central tank of the main corridor was reserved for a coelacanth, the famous living fossil that Earl Herald had long sought but, till then, had never obtained permission to capture. Elaborate mosaics by the artist William Wagner, one of many of Herald's admirers, were installed as a schematic to explain the aquarium's water systems to visitors. The star attraction was a large tank where, four times each day, dolphins and seals were fed by a soggy trainer and encouraged to jump as high as the adjoining rooftop.

San Francisco was once a major Pacific whaling port, and dolphins and whales had long been part of the Academy's legacy. The Academy's largest cetacean specimen was an eighty-six-foot skeleton of a blue whale suspended behind the Steinhart. It was captured in 1908 off Vancouver Island by the Pacific Whaling Company and provided millions of schoolchildren and park visitors with a chance to see the largest kind of mammal that has ever lived. Other whale sightings at the Academy included Pheena, a life-size fiberglass fin whale, and Sandy, a life-size gray whale, sculpted by Larry "General Whale" Foster, which graced the Academy's doorstep and were often coated with playful children.

Though dolphins were a favorite, a sirenian named Butterball, an Amazonian manatee, was probably the aquarium's most memorable mammal. Sirenians are so named because early mariners observed these robust, paddle-tailed aquatic mammals suckling their young and (although the animals were hardly attractive) thought that they had encountered mermaids. Academy trustee Wilson Meyer happened upon the ailing manatee for sale at a fish market in Colombia in 1967, ransomed the rotund beast, and somehow got it to San Francisco. For the next seventeen years, Butterball made history as one of the longest-lived Amazonian manatees in captivity. Most visitors considered Butterball

to be a mermaid, not a merman, despite the assertion in the adjacent caption that Butterball was male.

Following in the footsteps of his predecessor, Seale, Herald had occasional clashes with his superiors. Largely as a result of Herald's gregarious personality and his widespread television exposure, confusion existed in the public's mind as to who was in charge of that museum in Golden Gate Park. Most citizens called it "the Steinhart" or "the Aquarium," and visitors and chagrined Academy directors were often met by blank stares from cabbies when requesting a ride to the Academy of Sciences. But if they said "the Steinhart" or "the Aquarium," the response was inevitably, "Why didnya say so?" Herald apparently enjoyed the confusion. Academy executive director George E. Lindsay (1963 to 1982), a towering presence and no faint lily himself, sheepishly related an experience he'd had in 1971, when Charles Schroeder, upon his retirement as director of the world-famous San

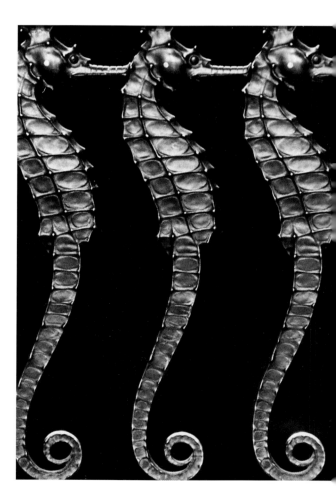

Diego Zoo, asked Lindsay's advice concerning a successor. Lindsay wasted no time in writing that he could think of no one as well qualified as Herald, only to be later told by Schroeder that he had received a nearly identical letter from Herald nominating Lindsay for the same job.

The Academy flourished, and San Francisco enjoyed both Steinhart director Herald and Academy executive director Lindsay. Herald received numerous awards and much recognition as his renovated aquarium attracted more than two million visitors each year. Then, in 1973, Herald met a tragic end at age fifty-nine in Baja California: he drowned while scuba diving in pursuit of his lifetime quarry, rare and exotic fish.

an EVOLVING MUSEUM When the Steinhart opened in 1923, at its entrance were three seal grottoes, accessible to the public during kinder and gentler times. The grottoes were replaced in the early 1950s with a memorial statue to Francis Scott Key, which was in turn replaced in 1957 with a fountain and black granite statue of two entwined whales at the center of the Academy's courtyard. Sculpted by Robert B. Howard in 1938, it had previously appeared as the centerpiece of the San Francisco Building at the Treasure Island 1939–1940 World's Fair.

The Academy's gift shop, at the entrance to the swamp, expanded in scope and philosophy in 1979 when the Nature Company Museum Store, headquartered in Berkeley, California, became its new proprietor. Its founders, Tom and Priscilla Wrubel, were pioneers in the merchandising of natural history items and had excellent taste and a strong conservation ethic. Another innovation, enjoyed by all who experienced them, were the tape-recorded tours, prepared by a theatrical company called Antenna Tours, which visitors could rent and listen to through headphones as they explored the exhibits. Now the standard of the industry, their first adventure as individually guided museum tours was at the Steinhart.

BELOW The bronze sea horse railing, surrounding the alligator swamp, has been an emblem of the Steinhart Aquarium since it was first built in 1923. The railing has been preserved in the new Academy, and new sea horses, identical to the originals, have been added to encircle a new, renovated swamp.

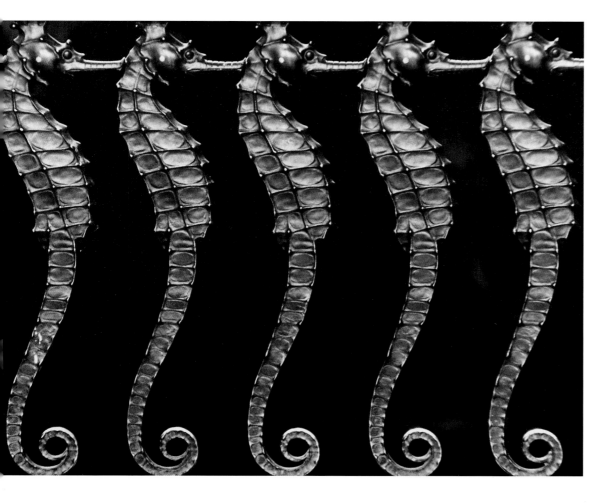

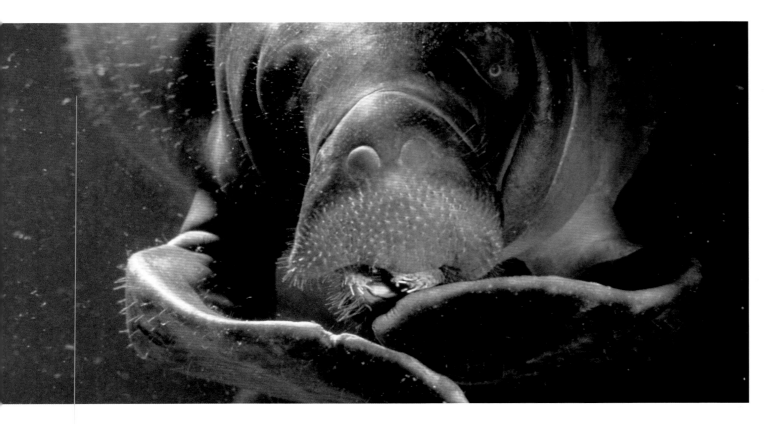

Academy director George Lindsay was responsible for numerous important additions during his tenure, including the return of anthropology as a discipline and exhibit topic at the Academy. At the onset of the twentieth century, the Academy had been poised to become a major center for anthropological research, with Alfred Kroeber on staff. But in 1901, after an argument with the board of directors (purportedly over his request for $50 for field expenses), Kroeber left the Academy to join UC Berkeley, where he became known as the "dean of American anthropologists," and that was the end of the discipline at the Academy. Lindsay was determined to provide visitors with exhibits about human cultures and the origin of mankind, and he convinced Mrs. Phyllis Wattis to support the creation of the Wattis Hall of Man. It opened in 1976 with ten open dioramas depicting eerily lifelike fiberglass castings of humans within various environments. With depictions ranging from Netsilik Eskimos to Micronesian islanders, New Guinea tribesmen, New World Hopi, and Andean villagers, each exhibit explained how humans have adapted to their environs and how cultures have adapted differently to similar challenges.

PASSION *for* SCIENCE My first day of work in 1973 as director of the Steinhart Aquarium was momentous. As I was being welcomed, a jogger with a pistol pointed at the comptroller was emptying the business office safe, marking the largest armed robbery in the Academy's history. Having survived earthquakes, the Depression, and 120 years of San Francisco politics and heretics, the Academy staff soon forgot the events of that day. But for me, it was the beginning of a two-decade love affair with fish and the people who enjoy them. I hired David Powell, the curator of the very successful Sea World oceanarium in San Diego, and we and the staff designed and built many new displays, including the novel Roundabout Tank. Most pelagic fishes neither comprehend nor tolerate confinement, and the result of placing a tuna or a thresher shark in a regular rectangular tank is a fish dead after colliding with the wall. The Roundabout, a cuboidal four-story structure housing a ring tank sixty feet in diameter and ten feet wide, allowed open-ocean, or pelagic, fishes to swim against a weak one-knot current through an infinite envelope of oceanic water.

Aquarium visitors entered the toroidal (doughnut-shaped) room encircled by the tank from

beneath and found themselves surrounded by fishes—striped bass, leopard sharks, seven-gill sharks, and more. Erupting from the center of the entry level of the Roundabout was the Touch Tank, a rocky, natural tide pool that allowed visitors to handle starfish, sea hares, algae, and crabs, which live in this wave-washed zone. Little did we expect that this "wet-hands laboratory" would become a "wet-carpet circus," with twenty-five thousand hands struggling each year to pet a sea urchin or squeeze a sea cucumber. The Roundabout, which opened in 1977, proved so popular that Academy attendance rocketed to 1.8 million that year. It also provided researchers and students with an opportunity to study oceanic creatures firsthand. Yellowtail serendipitously spawned, and species that had previously defied captivity, such as the large seven-gill sharks and soupfin sharks, swam happily around. And we nearly succeeded in being the first aquarium to maintain a healthy great white shark.

I am often asked, "What was the single most memorable event in your twenty-one years of running Steinhart Aquarium?" It would be difficult to pick one, were it not for Sandy, a seven-and-a-half-foot, 350-pound young female great white shark. Together, Sandy and the Steinhart amazed and educated hundreds of thousands of people and affected a sea change in the public's attitude about sharks. No healthy white shark had ever survived captivity, and after the film *Jaws* it became the holy grail of the aquarium world. Then, one day in 1980, a fisherman called from his boat off Bodega Bay and said he had one. The shark survived the convoluted transport to the Steinhart and was kept for four and a half days, swimming in the Roundabout and gazed upon by thousands. We were ecstatic but cautious, as Sandy occasionally had difficulty maneuvering a five-degree arc of the tank. Then we realized that Sandy was so electrosensitive, she was reacting, often violently, to an electrical leak from the rebar behind the tank's membrane. We decided to do something previously unimag-ined: we would release her back to the ocean rather than allow her to die in the tank. We took her to the Farallon Islands and watched her swim away. Although Sandy hadn't landed the record of the great white shark held longest in captivity, she was different: she was still alive. We took pride in the birth of an attitude—that if an animal is incapable of surviving in captivity, it should be released—that is now nearly universal.

ABOVE LEFT For many years the aquarium's most famous inhabitant was Butterball, an Amazonian manatee. This graceful, gentle herbivore—bought by an Academy trustee at a fish market in Columbia in 1967—was exhibited for seventeen years and became one of the longest-lived sirenians in captivity.

ABOVE Pelagic fish live in the open ocean and do not understand barriers; if you put them in a rectangular tank, they'll keep banging into the glass. The Steinhart's solution was to build a doughnut-shaped tank with water continuously flowing in one direction. Fish generally swim against the current, so tuna, jacks, sharks, and other pelagic fish were able to keep swimming in the Roundabout without ever colliding with the glass barriers.

1970s *and* 1980s During the 1970s, the Academy joined the nationwide trend of museums renting or creating temporary exhibitions. The long and wide-ranging list of Academy shows, beginning in 1974, includes such highlights as the Genius of Beniamino Bufano; Peru's Golden Treasures; Art of the First Australians; Hopi Kachina: Spirit of Life; Ice Age Art; Creativity, the Human Resource; Exploring the Deep Frontier; Roger Tory Peterson; the Unknown Ansel Adams; the Heritage of Islam; Photography of Imogen Cunningham; Andy Warhol: Endangered Species; the Art of Robert Bateman; the Great Central Valley; Fly Fishing; a series of Dinofests; Sliding toward Extinction: The Vanishing Wildlife of California; Deserts;

Star Trek: Federation Science; and a variety of natural history exhibits involving bats, monarch butterflies, venoms, skulls, fish X-rays, chocolate, amber, and ants.

An unexpected and extraordinary success was the Far Side of Science exhibit, a collection of Gary Larson cartoons with accompanying natural-history explanations that premiered at the Academy in 1985. It began with the Run to the Far Side, a 5K and 10K race through San Francisco's Panhandle neighborhood and Golden Gate Park. The exhibit, after traveling across the United States and Canada, returned to become a permanent installation within the Academy, and the race became an annual tradition.

The Academy also hosted regular programs and events over the years, such as the annual High School Science Fair, the Fungus Fair, the meetings of the San Francisco Aquarium Society, the Herbst Lecture Programs, and the annual St. Patrick's Day Snake Race. Its popular Junior Academy, which the Academy hosted each weekend and throughout the summer, educated and inspired such youngsters as Peter Raven, who went on to become the director of the Missouri Botanical Garden and the secretary of the National Academy of Sciences.

Before George Lindsay retired, he commissioned long-term studies of the Academy's scientific mission and a master plan for its future. They were undertaken by J. C. Dickinson, of Florida State Museum, and by the McKinsey Company and were completed in 1980. The advice proved so valuable that two of the McKinsey consultants, John W. Larson and Thomas B. Klein, ultimately became trustees of the Academy. (Larson, who had advised large institutions around the world, observed with a grimace that understanding the Academy was as complicated as managing General Motors.)

The studies reaffirmed that having an aquarium, a planetarium, and a natural history museum under the same roof was key to the Academy's success. The movement and vitality that living creatures provide to otherwise static exhibits made the Academy a special destination. And soon after his arrival, Frank Hamilton Talbot (1982 to 1988), George Lindsay's successor, began to include aquarium displays beyond the historic footprint of the Steinhart.

In 1988, North American Hall, which had remained largely unchanged for six decades, except for occasional updating of the legends as species became uncommon or nearly extinct, underwent major renovation. Its exhibit, including a fourteen-thousand-gallon Farallon Islands aquarium tank, was renamed Wild California: A State of Diversity, and the building was renamed Meyer Hall, in honor of the project's primary donor, Jeffery W. Meyer. A grizzly bear was placed at the entrance, and several life-size sculpted elephant seals, with a soundtrack of their snorts and grunts, were center stage on the floor. The grizzly, named Monarch, was thought to be the last one captured in California. Caught and put on display in 1889, it died in 1911, was taxidermied by the M. H. de Young Memorial Museum staff, and acquired by the Academy in 1953. Monarch's fame then grew exponentially when Don Greame Kelley, founding editor of the Academy's magazine *Pacific Discovery*, was commissioned to redesign the California state flag, upon which Monarch now proudly resides.

Life Through Time: The Evidence for Evolution opened in 1989 in the McBean-Peterson galleries. Open dioramas with animated dinosaurs and giant insects, along with live and preserved reptiles, fish, and invertebrates, demonstrated the living links in the evolution of life. These displays, along with interactive computer games and other onscreen information, made the Academy a showpiece for other museums to emulate.

At the aquarium, which has been home to more than ten thousand individuals of nearly five hundred species, ranging from microscopic brine shrimp to megascopic crocodiles, few animals have ever been lost. A few, however, are cryptic, shy, and difficult to keep track of. Despite our best efforts, one occasionally was unaccounted for. Lloyd Gomez, the enthusiastic aquatic biologist who oversaw the marine displays, thought that he had constructed an enclosure from which no reptilian Papillon could ever escape. But at the end of one day, a camouflaged banded sea snake was unaccounted for. Where was it? At the back of the 650-gallon tank, it was discovered that the screen normally covering a one-inch-diameter drain hole was missing. The drain line led to filters, which had an overflow to the sewer. Our best guess was that the sea snake was heading downhill to the Richmond-Sunset Sewage Treatment Plant, a long, cold underground run that a tropical Philippine snake probably wouldn't survive. I nervously phoned the head of the sewage plant to warn him of the remote possibility of a visit. He assured me the snake couldn't get past the screens or the digesters, but if it did he would call. The snake was never seen again.

LOMA PRIETA *and the* FUTURE Soon after his arrival as executive director, Roy Eisenhardt (1989 to 1994) and the Bay Area were greeted by the October 17, 1989, Loma Prieta earthquake. Although the Academy did not suffer significant damage—library shelves collapsed, the Cowell Hall entrance suffered

structural damage, and Bird Hall was rendered unusable—the various buildings that had been juxtaposed over the years were showing their age. The Steinhart, the oldest still-operating aquarium in the United States, needed serious attention. It was time for serious reconstruction.

The combination of an aquarium, planetarium, and natural history museum is what makes the Academy unique. In order to continue educating visitors on-site and beyond, the Academy's board of trustees was faced with a major decision: renovate or rebuild? After long and arduous study, the board chose to completely rebuild, taking advantage of what it had learned and accomplished since the Academy's opening.

Just as its various living and re-created displays have been key to the Academy's success, so have the intertwined facets of the Academy's mission—to explore, explain, and protect the natural world. The original purpose of the Academy, to discover and document the kinds and abundance of life on the Pacific Coast, is still high among its goals, but its scope has been expanded over the years to embrace all life on Earth. The presence of staff researchers has provided real-time explanation of scientific discoveries from all over the world, an audit of the accuracy of the Academy's presentations to the public, and finally, critical input into the choices that inevitably must be made about which species and environments can and must be protected. Recognizing the subtle differences among species requires the skill and training of systematic biologists whose knowledge informs other scientists who work with plants and animals. Little of life on Earth is currently catalogued (estimates range as low as 10 percent), and far less is adequately understood. As habitats disappear, so do the species that rely on them. Nineteenth-century Academy scientists focused on California and Mexico. Twentieth-century researchers broadened their scope to include the Galápagos Islands and other outposts throughout the globe, above and below water. Academy researchers today focus on global hot spots—China, Myanmar, Madagascar, the Galápagos, and the Philippines— where known and unknown plants and animals will be extinct before you have finished reading this chapter.

Past and continuing studies by the aquarium staff have concerned the biology of threatened and endangered species, as well as studies of fish, penguin, and cetacean behaviors. Aquarium research expeditions have returned with flash-light fishes, frozen coelacanths, great white sharks, and humming toadfishes. Breeding programs have involved rare and endangered red-legged frogs, Francisco garter snakes, giant sea horses, black-footed penguins, American desert pupfishes, African cichlid fishes, and winter-run Chinook salmon.

The protection of the Earth's endangered resources and ecosystems is informed directly and indirectly by the exploration and education activities of the Academy. The Academy has played a critical role in helping to establish protection for gray whales and great white sharks and for ecosystems such as those of Mount Shasta, the Farallon Islands, and Big Basin Redwoods preserve.

Since opening day in 1916, more than 125 million visitors have marveled at the Academy's fascinating fish and displays. Nearly every schoolchild in San Francisco and most from the surrounding communities have visited at least once, and many visit every year. We've also been visited by presidents and governors, every San Francisco mayor from Sunny Jim Rolph to Gavin Newsom, actors and actresses (including Raymond Burr, who grew up in the Avenues and applied for, but didn't get, an aquarist's job), rock stars and Oakland Raiderettes, Prince Charles (who went shark fishing on the bay for Steinhart specimens), heads of state (and amateur ichthyologists) such as Emperor Akihito of Japan and President Chadli Bendjedid of Algeria, and spiritual leaders, including His Holiness the Dalai Lama. But we have never differentiated our public. In the eyes of the fish, all visitors are the same.

Dr. John E. McCosker is a senior scientist and the chair of Aquatic Biology at the California Academy of Sciences.

PART 1

BUILDING
A VISION

This wooden architectural model of the Academy's undulating roof was used by the Renzo Piano Building Workshop to study the geometry of the new building's domes and piazza.

CH 1 Fourteen million insects and arachnids, two million jarred fish specimens, ten thousand sets of delicate bird nests and eggs, five hundred Japanese folk toys, platypus skulls, stuffed bats and giraffes, six-foot-long pile worms, whale and rhinoceros bones, more than five thousand living fish, penguins, serpents, and other creatures—a library of life on Earth fills the collections and exhibits of the California Academy of Sciences. And in 2004, when the museum left its eighty-eight-year home in San Francisco's Golden Gate Park, it faced the confounding challenge of packing and transporting its vast, often irreplaceable contents three miles away to a temporary site across the city.

No natural history museum in the world had ever made such a massive move. With millions of fragile scientific specimens—some tiny, some gigantic, and many the only examples of their kind in the entire world—the transfer took expert handling and creativity. In each of the Academy's research departments, trained teams swaddled drawers of specimens in bubble wrap, cotton, and foam,

then carefully transported the sealed cabinets to the museum's interim quarters at 875 Howard Street. Construction crews razed walls to transfer some of the biggest specimens, including dolphins preserved in huge vats of alcohol. Meanwhile, live aquarium animals made the move, one or a few at a time, on stretchers or in ice chests, burlap sacks, Styrofoam boxes, cloth bags, water-filled shipping containers, or socks. Although the patient packing and transporting of specimens and living creatures seemed never-ending, the move was completed successfully, with no major losses, in just five months.

NEW FOCUS *on* CHANGE For a natural history museum, whose exhibits can seem frozen in time, the disruption of the move was transformational. Since the nineteenth century, when many natural history museums were founded, these institutions had become known mainly for fixed dioramas, stuffed creatures, and arcane collections hidden from public view. In the twenty-first century, however, natural history museums, like all scientific institutions, need to focus on change, according

to Gregory Farrington, the Academy of Sciences' executive director. "Science moves quickly," he says, "and institutions that are talking about science need to move quickly, too. The California Academy of Sciences is not only a home for specimens—it's a leading intellectual institution with a global presence. It needs to focus on the future, not just the past."

In a fast-changing world, where people can instantly access facts and virtual experiences through a computer, the role of a natural history museum has to be reimagined. "We can no longer passively present specimens of life on Earth," Farrington says. "Our challenge and our opportunity are to introduce people to the amazing, real-life wonders of the natural world and to stir their emotions so they care deeply about its survival. The dynamic of change has moved to the front burner, and a change of place is a good way to change everything we do."

CRUMBLING INFRASTRUCTURE Physically, too, the move was necessary. The oldest scientific institution in the West, the Academy of Sciences had been in Golden

Gate Park since 1916. The wear and tear of passing decades, and of more than a hundred million visitors, had taken a toll. The Academy's sixty-six-year-old Steinhart Aquarium, five major exhibit halls, thirty-seven-year-old Morrison Planetarium, and buildings for collections and research were already suffering from crumbling concrete, sagging floors, cracked walls, leaks, peeling paint, and corrosion when the 7.1-magnitude Loma Prieta earthquake struck the city on October 17, 1989. The seventy-three-year-old Bird Hall was damaged beyond repair, and other buildings—including African Hall and the Steinhart Aquarium—were unstable and unlikely to survive another major quake.

To fund critical repairs, the Steinhart and Academy of Sciences turned to the voters of San Francisco. In November 1993, Proposition A, an omnibus bill, sought to raise $98 million for nine art and culture projects, including $22 million to renovate the damaged aquarium. Passage of the bond, however, required a two-thirds majority, and although 61.2 percent of city voters supported it, the measure failed.

FAR LEFT By 1954, the Academy of Sciences complex in Golden Gate Park included African Hall (left) and North American Mammals Hall (right), which flanked the Morrison Planetarium and the Steinhart Aquarium. The statue of Francis Scott Key, author of "The Star-Spangled Banner," was later moved to the Concourse.

LEFT Demolition begins on the old Academy in Golden Gate Park in 2004.

Two years later, the California Academy of Sciences went back to city voters, this time alone, to raise money for an increasingly urgent overhaul of the aquarium's disintegrating infrastructure, including all the concrete and life-support systems for fish and other marine life. In November 1995, Proposition C—a $29 million bond issue—aimed to finance those renovations, plus lead and asbestos abatement and improvements in access for the disabled. The measure won strong support from scientists, educators, community leaders, the Board of Supervisors, former mayors, and mayoral candidates, and it passed with landslide approval by more than 80 percent of city voters.

With this outpouring of popular support and with funding in hand, the Academy prepared to move forward with plans to retrofit and rebuild the aquarium. Those preparations were abruptly halted the next year, however, when the city's new mayor, Willie Brown, proposed that the Academy and the M. H. de Young Memorial Museum—its neighboring institution in Golden Gate Park—relocate downtown. The de Young, like the Academy of Sciences, needed major repairs to fix earthquake damage and aging infrastructure. Instead of rebuilding the institutions where they were, however, Mayor Brown—pressured by citizens who wanted to restrict automobile traffic in the park—suggested a plan to move both museums to the empty Transbay Terminal building at Mission and First Streets. In this shared downtown location, near Yerba Buena Gardens and the San Francisco Museum of Modern Art, they could help create a new cultural corridor in the city. There was widespread public opposition to the move, however, and by 1998 Mayor Brown had dropped the relocation plan, committing instead to revitalizing long-neglected Golden Gate Park and its cultural attractions.

TAKING STOCK The two-year interruption was a turning point for the Academy. Instead of proceeding with piecemeal repairs of existing buildings, the museum's board and staff began to take stock of fundamental issues concerning the Academy's future. In 1998, Patrick Kociolek, an Academy scientist, was named interim director and subsequently executive director of the

institution. With the board of trustees, he led nearly two years of wide-ranging discussions about the Academy's vision. "We urged everybody to rethink everything," recals Richard Bingham, who served as chairman of the board from 1996 to 2007. "'What is a natural history and science museum in the twenty-first century?' That was the real question," Kociolek adds. "The old-style natural history museum was built around the idea that there were some eternal truths about science and geography. But science changes, and places evolve culturally, biologically, and geologically."

Presentation modes needed to change, too, since attendance at natural history museums had been declining for twenty years. "We had a new generation of learners about the natural world," Kociolek says, "and we needed to find ways to bring them—and their parents—back into the museum." To do that, the Academy needed to confer with scientific experts about future directions in marine biology, geology, and biodiversity, as well as in the aquarium world and at NASA. Over the course of eighteen months, the Academy held intensive community

OPPOSITE PAGE In 2000, Mayor Willie Brown helped kick off the Yes on B campaign on the steps of the Academy of Sciences. Over two-thirds of San Francisco voters approved the city's bond measure for $87 million to reconstruct portions of the institution.

conversations—more than 150 focus groups with trustees, staff, Academy members, Bay Area residents, schoolchildren, scientists from around the world, and museum professionals—about what the California Academy of Sciences could become.

In the course of those dialogues, it became clear to the board that the existing facilities could no longer support the Academy's vision. "Simply upgrading the physical plant was not going to do it," Kociolek says. "Science is about challenging dogma, but our infrastructure was not about change. It was about marble, glass, and brass for housing dioramas."

Space was also too tight to accommodate growing collections, and the Academy's layout kept scientists isolated from one another and out of sight—and reach—of museum visitors. "The issues that science is trying to address today are interdisciplinary," Kociolek adds, "and it's crucial for us to make the science we do more accessible to the public. People are being called on to make so many more decisions on crucial questions involving the world's environment and resources, and scientists ought to be more helpful than ever in providing answers."

a WORLD-CLASS MUSEUM Instead of repairing its antiquated structures, the Academy's board decided to start from the ground up and build a new facility that would meet its mission and its changing needs in the twenty-first century. "Our goal was to build a world-class building that would house a set of world-class programs and people," Bingham explains. Given the complexity of the Academy's scope—as the nation's only combined natural history museum, aquarium, planetarium, and research institution—we also needed to find a world-class architect."

To begin the search, the board formed an architectural committee and invited thirty-five of the world's most renowned architects to submit designs for the selection process. The committee narrowed that field to six and ultimately three architects, whom they invited to San Francisco in 1999 for formal interviews. After the first two architects had made elaborate presentations with

BELOW This early concept sketch by architect
Renzo Piano shows the integration of the new
Academy's programming, art, exhibits, and
central piazza with natural lighting and the
park environment.

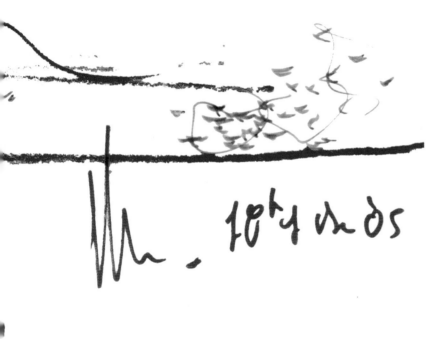

highly developed concepts for the new Academy, committee members met with the final candidate, Renzo
Piano. The winner of the 1998 Pritzker Architecture Prize,
Piano had previously designed Paris's Centre Pompidou
and Berlin's Potsdamer Platz. Despite his reputation,
however, Piano arrived without attitude or entourage,
equipped only with a sketch pad and a green felt-tip pen.
"Instead of explaining his design for the new building,"
Bingham says, "Renzo simply asked us about our hopes
and dreams for the new Academy." As the committee
talked, often passionately, about the project, the architect sketched.

"That day, the committee and I spent two hours together,"
Piano remembers. "I wanted to hear them talk about
science, about the spirit of the place. For me, at the
beginning of any job, it's important to listen." Soon after-
ward, the architecture committee voted unanimously to
select Renzo Piano and began a collaborative process of
dialogue, creative exploration, and design.

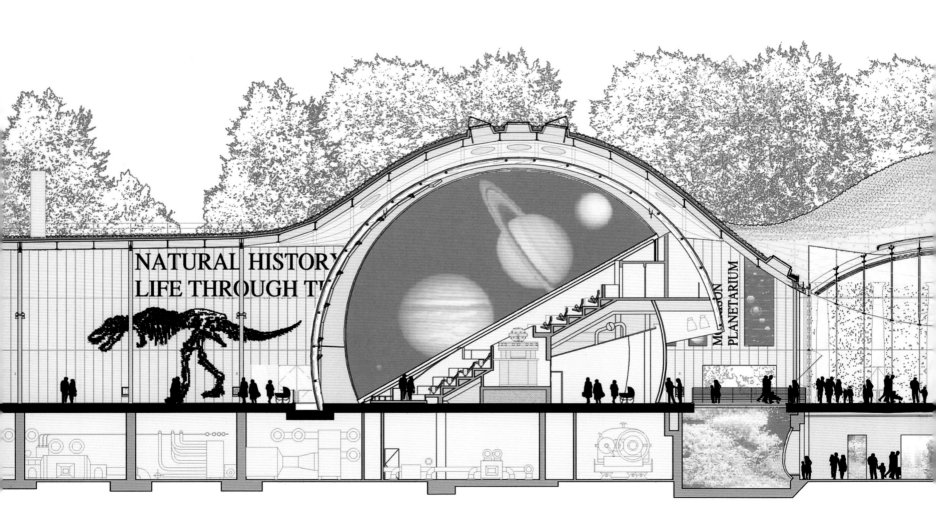

This cross section, looking south, shows the planetarium dome, exhibit hall, piazza, and rainforest dome of the new Academy, as well as skylights that naturally vent warm air through the roof.

NATURAL HISTORY
LIFE THROUGH T

M   ON
PLANETARIUM

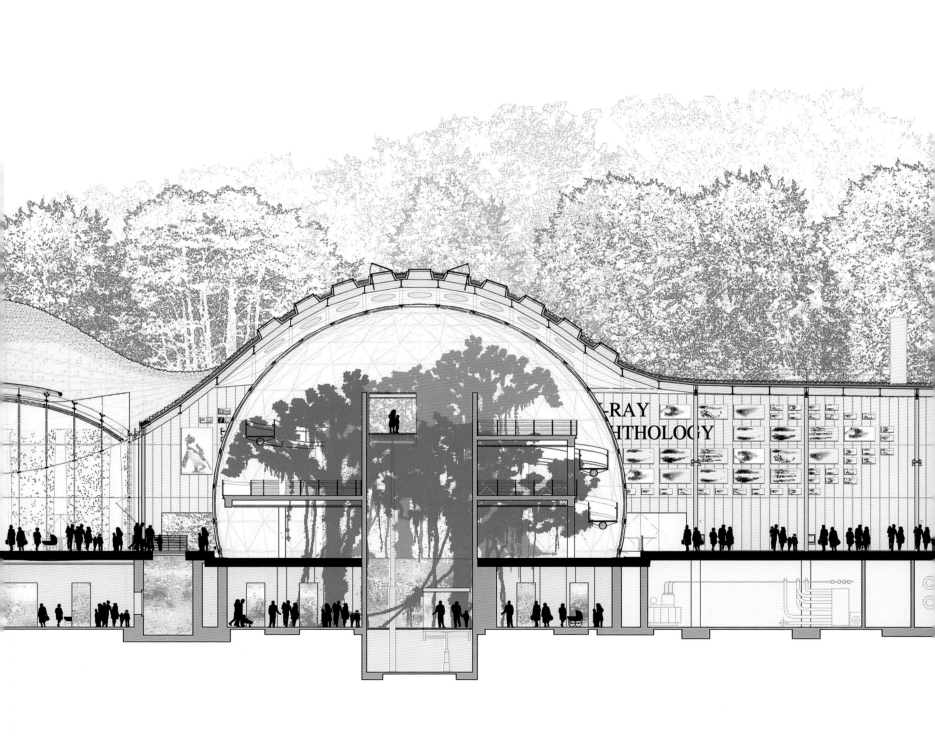

BUILDING *the* FUTURE Cost studies had shown that it would be less expensive to build a new facility than to renovate existing buildings. Still, it was clear that the project would take more money than the 1995 city bond measure had raised. In March 2000, the Academy went back to San Francisco voters with a new $87 million proposition to reconstruct parts of the institution. Boosted by voters' strong support for the museum, the measure won the two-thirds majority that it needed to pass. With new confidence and $122 million in bond money, plus $20 million from the State of California, the board then launched a drive to raise additional funds from private sources to finance a complete rebuilding. "The Academy had never had a history of large fundraising campaigns," Bingham remembers, "and trustees were worried. But I've always believed that if you have a good product, you can find the money for it. I said, 'Let's focus on building a first-class building—if we do that, we'll raise the funds.'"

No one yet knew what the building would look like. There was wide agreement, however, that the new Academy should reimagine the tradition of natural history institutions and serve as a role model and inspiration for museum design. From the start, Academy planners knew that they would not just tear down the old building and put up a replica in its place, with separate halls and exhibit areas. They envisioned, instead, an open museum without halls, a place that integrated research, education, and exhibits. "We needed to shake things up," Kociolek says. "Today, families have more time demands and many more choices than ever before—and with technology, people don't even need to leave their homes to get information. That's why we needed to build a place that people will want to come back to, with exciting approaches that change frequently, reflect current science, and enrich the visitor experience as much as possible."

The new Academy, all agreed, should also reflect and integrate the world outside, including the natural environment and landscape of Golden Gate Park. "The tendency is for natural history institutions to be inward, but that's exactly the wrong way to think about a science museum," Bingham observes. "The old Academy was like a black

MIDDLE Scientists gently cradle a blacktip shark in a canvas sling, before placing it in a tank on a truck and moving it downtown. Before the old Academy could be demolished, all specimens, living and dead, had to be moved to temporary quarters on Howard Street.

FAR RIGHT A child gazes through a window in the temporary coral reef tank in the Academy's Howard Street site, which drew more than a million visitors between 2003 and 2008.

box, but the new museum needed to be transparent—to be open to its setting and to people, information, and ideas." Research, too, would be transformed in the new building. "We needed a facility that could keep scientists connected to visitors and to one another," Kociolek says, "a building that creates spaces for the people who make up the Academy's intellectual capital to come together, interact, and create dialogue and that brings the public into the process of discovery."

GREEN DESIGN It was also a given that the building should be at the forefront of "green" building design, reflecting the Academy's ethic of environmental efficiency, conservation, and sustainability. Environmental concerns, Kociolek notes, date back to the museum's founding. The Academy of Sciences was established, in part, in response to the deforestation of much of the Gold Country during the gold rush. The Academy was also the first home of the Sierra Club, and it helped establish Yosemite National Park and Big Basin, the first state park in California. The goal for the new Academy, Kociolek

says, was to inspire a profound connection to and respect for the living world. It would showcase world-class architecture that fully integrates green building features and would set a new standard for sustainable design. "Global temperatures are rising, the rate of species extinctions is climbing, and natural resources are being consumed more rapidly than ever before," Kociolek explains. "Everyone agreed that as we began to build our new home in Golden Gate Park, we would be committed to using design and construction strategies that protect the natural world."

Over the next three years, in extensive dialogues with the Academy, Renzo Piano architecturally responded to these needs. He developed plans for a bold, organic design, rooted in memory and bathed in light, that "breathes" with the park, beckons visitors, and embodies energy-efficient, environmentally sustainable approaches to building design and construction. Under a living roof, planted with nearly two million native California plants, the new Academy of Sciences would bring together a reinvented natural history museum; a new immersive,

digital planetarium; new aquarium exhibits, including a three-story living rainforest and the deepest living-coral-reef tank in the world; a hands-on naturalist center; research laboratories accessible to the public; and immense collections. The spirit of the new design, Piano says, is to announce and enforce the Academy's complexity of function in a simple, minimal, flexible space that connects almost seamlessly with the natural landscape.

the UN-MUSEUM There was nothing simple, however, about the process of dismantling and vacating the old Academy to begin construction. The process was like "a fast-moving train," says Alison Brown, chief financial and operations officer, who managed the organizational aspects of the project from concept to completion. On December 31, 2003, the Academy of Sciences closed the doors of its quake-cracked buildings and began the monumental transfer of eighteen million specimens and more than five thousand living creatures from Golden Gate Park to its interim location downtown, on Howard Street. The six-story, 217,000-square-foot

FAR LEFT Mock-ups permitted the architects and Webcor Builders, the Academy's general contractor, to experiment, test ideas, and save time and money. This roof mock-up tested the structural steel, decking, skylights, water-proofing, soil, and plants used in the design and construction of the living roof.

ABOVE This view from the deYoung Museum, located opposite the Academy, across the Music Concourse, shows the site following demolition and midway through excavation.

LEFT This mock-up tested glass systems used in the exhibit hall and the piazza, as well as the color and finish of the building's concrete.

ABOVE Construction crews complete the canopy framing for the solar panels.

RIGHT One of the two preserved walls of African Hall is braced by steel supports during demolition.

OPPOSITE PAGE A web of rebar and conduit criss-crosses forms for the roof skylights.

space—formerly a department store warehouse—was soon outfitted with interactive industrial displays featuring exposed pipes and valves, a two-story fish tank and coral nursery, penguins and snakes, live ant and astrobiology exhibits, a library and naturalist center, a children's play area, a café and retail store, and research and storage facilities. For three and a half years, the temporary site served as a lab, enabling the Academy to experiment with flexible new exhibit and working styles, and it drew more than a million visitors. "In many ways," Kociolek says, "the Howard Street site exceeded our expectations. The downtown location made the Academy more accessible to people, and we developed a new audience while staying in the public eye."

Few, however, regretted the closure of the temporary museum in early January 2008 and the "great migration" of millions of priceless treasures and living creatures back to Golden Gate Park. The eight-month parade of painstakingly packed specimens concluded in time for the autumn 2008 opening of the Academy of Sciences' brand-new home.

The new building, Gregory Farrington says, marks the evolution of the Academy from an assemblage of natural history exhibits and specimens to an international center for scientific education and research at the forefront of efforts to understand and protect the diversity of Earth's living things.

"The new Academy is the 'un-museum,'" Farrington states. "So many museums are Greek revival, with high staircases and dark corridors. This is the inverse of that—we've turned the museum inside out, with glass walls and open space. The building is flooded with light, not closed in. The architectural statement is all about life inside and around the institution. It's a showcase for life—how we got here, its amazing diversity, and how we're going to stay."

It's also, he adds, one of the boldest public-private investments of wealth in a Bay Area cultural institution. Starting with a generous lead gift from former board chairman William Kimball, the Academy has raised more than $430 million, mainly from private sources. As a

result, Farrington says, the reinvented California Academy of Sciences is, in every way, an exhibit in itself of what is possible.

"We are creating a new model for how institutions of this sort can be successful, serve their communities, and engage and educate the public," Farrington adds. "This institution and the causes that it represents are global, and its intellectual leadership will be global in scope and vision. We are just at the very beginning of this new adventure. The building sets the stage—now comes the play."

ABOVE LEFT Construction workers erect the structural steel framing for the "hills" on the Academy's roof.

ABOVE RIGHT Crews from Jensen, the Academy's landscape contractor, install planted trays over a layer of loose soil on the Academy's roof.

BELOW This photograph, taken from the tower of the deYoung Museum midway through construction, shows the Academy's roof with filter fabric partially installed to collect particulates from storm-water runoff. The Academy's green roof absorbs 98 percent of all storm-water flows, keeping up to two million gallons of runoff per year out of the city's drains.

The skylight system over the Academy's central piazza is engineered to provide sunlight, shade, rain protection, and acoustic buffering depending on changes in the weather and the courtyard's use.

CH 2 Architects, says Renzo Piano, use a physical alphabet, a language of structure and form. "We tell stories through architecture," he says, and those stories are changing. Instead of a narrative about style—neo-Romantic, for example, or neo-Gothic—architects are now learning to tell a new story "about nature and the fragility of the world around us. Even our alphabet is new," he adds. "It is no longer about formal academic trends, but about natural materials, lightness, and sensitivity."

With the new California Academy of Sciences, Piano has designed a museum that is visually and functionally linked to its natural surroundings, metaphorically lifting up a piece of the park and inserting a building beneath. The new design unifies the Academy's original array of twelve buildings, built over eight decades, into a single, more compact modern landmark that returns an acre of land to the park and places a visual and intellectual emphasis on the natural world. "The building and the park breathe together," Piano says, with a free flow of light, air, and crystalline views.

BELOW The piazza's "spiderweb" of delicate steel
rods and fittings supports a system of retractable
fabric sun, rain, and acoustic screens.

Unlike the dark halls and "cabinets of curiosities" that have traditionally characterized natural history museums, the new Academy's galleries are open, airy, and bursting with light and life. By optimizing the use of resources and minimizing environmental impacts, the Academy is also helping to set a new standard for energy efficiency and environmentally sensitive engineering. Through ecologically minded architecture and innovative design, the building embodies the Academy's dedication to environmental responsibility, which begins with a responsible approach to its own environment.

"Science is more influential and relevant to our daily lives than ever before," says Gregory Farrington, "and natural history museums can and must deal head-on with the issues of the twenty-first century. Our goal was to create a new facility that will not only hold powerful exhibits but also serve as one itself, inspiring visitors to conserve natural resources and help sustain the diversity of life on Earth."

TRANSPARENCY *and* CONNECTION "Museums are not usually transparent," Piano explains. "They are opaque and closed. They are like a kingdom of darkness, and you are trapped inside." In the old Academy, he adds, "you were in the middle of Golden Gate Park, one of the most beautiful places in the world, but you didn't see where you were and had no sense of what was there."

In his architectural design for the new building, Piano wanted to create a feeling of transparency and connection between the Academy and the park through careful attention to materials, landscaping, and the arrangement of space. The soaring glass exterior walls offer expansive views out to Golden Gate Park and, for those outside, into the exhibition galleries along both the east-west and north-south axes of the building. The superclear glass, which contains very little tint-producing iron, creates minimal color distortion. Unbroken views through the building extend across the park's Music Concourse to the new de Young museum (opened in 2005 and designed by Swiss architects Herzog and de Meuron), and foster an architectural dialogue between the buildings.

LINKS *to the* PAST The new building also creates a dialogue between past and present. "I like the tension between old and new," Piano says, "and when I first saw the original Academy, I felt a sense of history." Memory played a part in his design. Originally, the Academy was an organic collection of buildings, "like a village," he explains, with a large open courtyard in the center. The new Academy maintains that collective complexity. Its four wings, like four legs of a table, surround a light-filled central piazza that serves as a space where people can gather and mingle. "The Academy is still like a village," Piano says, with links to the past.

Those links were important to the architect. From the start, he wanted to preserve visual symbols of the Steinhart Aquarium and the classical structures that flanked the main entrance to the Academy. "African Hall was a piece of the past," he explains. "People were in love with that building, and I felt that immediately. The

aquarium, too, was a piece of history—not a building, but a place: chaotic, messy, rich, and meaningful." To preserve visual ties to the Academy's history, the architects retained two exterior walls of African Hall. They made casts of its elaborate ceiling tiles and other rich architectural details, and they carefully photographed the painted backgrounds of its dioramas. They also made castings from the capital columns that originally marked the entrance to the Steinhart Aquarium and rebuilt the swamp—one of the Steinhart's best-loved attractions—using its original sea horse railing and historic tiles.

Piano also preserved the original height of the Academy's facade. "The scale was quite good below the trees," he says, "and I felt that the new building should not be more than that. We very carefully measured the height from the ground to the cornice of the existing facade and replicated it exactly—not just to be obedient, but to preserve the proportion and keep close to the original inspiration of the institution." Maintaining a visual connection to the past is important, Piano says, because people sometimes emotionally adopt places and

RENZO PIANO : ARCHITECT *as* EXPLORER

By any measure, Renzo Piano stands among the world's greatest architects. His past projects include the Centre Pompidou in Paris, the Menil Collection Museum in Houston, the Beyeler Foundation Museum in Basel, the Kansai Air Terminal in Osaka, the New York Times Building in New York City, and the reconstruction of Berlin's Potsdamer Platz. He is currently working on designs for the Art Institute of Chicago, the Los Angeles County Museum of Art, the Whitney Museum of American Art in New York, the Isabella Stewart Gardner Museum in Boston, the Pierpont Morgan Library in New York, and London's Tower Bridge. In 1998, Piano was awarded the Pritzker Architecture Prize, regarded as the architectural equivalent of the Nobel.

Born in Genoa, Italy, in 1937, Piano often points to his father as his original inspiration. The Italian builder took his young son to the harbor to watch ships arrive, and Renzo saw them "as immense buildings that moved through space." Throughout his career, he carried this image of buildings "as structures that fight against gravity, miracles bending the laws of physics."

Architects, Piano says, are explorers. "Every place is different, every client is different, every society is different. Culturally, historically, psychologically, anthropologically, and topographically, every job is different. I try to understand what is the real nature of a place, what is the context." His buildings exhibit a sensitivity for the design, context, habitability, and sustainability of structures. As the jury awarding him the Pritzker Prize commented, "Piano achieves a rare melding of art, architecture, and engineering in a truly remarkable synthesis. He celebrates structure in a perfect union of technology and art."

buildings. "When you make a new building, you have to be careful" he explains. "It can be fantastic, it can be crisp and new, but it might not be loved."

a GREEN MUSEUM Green approaches were part of the design from the beginning. The Academy's mission is to explore, explain, and protect the natural world, and, according to Patrick Kociolek, the Academy's former executive director, "the board felt that there is no more important place to live up to those ideals than in our own building." Piano's firm, the Renzo Piano Building Workshop, collaborated closely with Stantec Architecture and consulting engineers from Arup to reinvent the Academy using energy-efficient, environmentally sensitive construction technologies that help preserve the natural integrity of the park environment, conserve water and energy, reduce pollution, and maximize natural light and ventilation inside. The result is a new 409,000-square-foot facility that sets a new sustainable-design standard for museums.

Green strategies began with the demolition of the old buildings and the selection of building materials for the new one. All demolition waste from the old Academy was recycled, including 12,000 tons of metal; 9,000 tons of concrete, which were reused for road construction; and 120 tons of green waste, used primarily for mulch and compost within the park. In addition, 80,000 tons of sand were recycled for restoration of dunes in and around Baker Beach; for replanting native vegetation at Land's End; for reuse by quarries in asphalt or direct sale; and as general fill for construction purposes at nearby sites. The designers also used recycled, renewable, and nontoxic materials in construction. All the structural steel used in the building is recycled, and at least 50 percent of the wood used was sustainably harvested and certified by the Forest Stewardship Council. All the concrete in the building contains at least 30 percent replacement material, including slag and fly ash (a by-product of coal-fired power plants), and even the insulation used in the building's walls is manufactured from recycled denim. Paints, adhesives, sealants, and carpets are made from

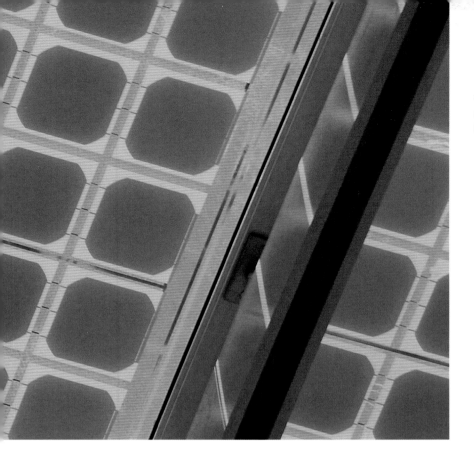

LEFT Photovoltaic cells embedded in the roof's canopy generate almost 213,000 kilowatt hours of clean energy per year.

low-emitting, nontoxic, environmentally safe materials, and the Academy is using green cleaning and pesticide-free landscape management programs.

ENERGY EFFICIENCY Natural lighting and ventilation are key strategies for reducing energy consumption and creating healthful, comfortable public and staff spaces. The building's glazed, transparent facades and roof sections allow daylight to filter into office, research, and exhibition areas: daylight illuminates 90 percent of the public spaces and 75 percent of all regularly occupied research and office areas, thereby helping to reduce energy use and heat gain from electric lighting. High-efficiency light fixtures and shorter wiring routes further conserve energy, and automatic controls minimize the overall use of artificial lights.

The Academy building, in fact, functions like a smart green machine that monitors its own lighting and temperature. Advanced photosensors in the lighting system automatically dim artificial lights in response to daylight penetration, reducing the need for electric lighting

RIGHT Acoustic and solar shades are extended in the central piazza to modulate sound and light.

BELOW In the ceiling of the exhibit hall, acoustic panels—which Renzo Piano likes to call "fish scales"—follow the undulations of the building's roof.

OPPOSITE PAGE The glass canopy extending from the roof's perimeter creates shaded shelter for Academy visitors.

in interior spaces. Motorized windows, louvers, and sky-lights—connected to sensors that detect indoor and outdoor temperature, sun position and intensity, wind speed and direction, and barometric pressure—automatically open and close to regulate the building's temperature. Staff offices have both automatic and easy-to-open manually operated windows, to keep work spaces comfortable, and the large, open piazza brings more natural light and ventilation to the museum's interior. A system of retractable fabric screens, supported by a "spiderweb" of delicate stainless-steel rods and construction fittings, keeps the partially covered courtyard comfortable in both sun and rain.

Exterior walls that are sixteen to eighteen inches thick absorb heat, creating a thermal lag that helps moderate the temperature inside, and radiant floor heating and cooling reduces energy needs up to 10 percent over what conventional techniques would require. Heat-recovery systems capture and use heat from the floor heating, ventilation system, and air-conditioning equipment, further reducing the amount of energy needed to moderate

interior temperatures. High-performance glass, used throughout the building, reduces heat absorption. High-pressure humidification systems keep research collections at a constant humidity level and reduce the energy necessary for humidification by 95 percent.

In the roof are 60,000 multicrystalline photovoltaic cells—the most energy-efficient cells on the market—which supply almost 213,000 kilowatt hours of clean energy per year. They also prevent the release of more than 405,000 pounds of greenhouse gasses, equivalent to the planting of more than 340 trees. As a result of all these strategies, the new Academy uses 30 percent less energy than the maximum allowed by the State of California.

Construction of the new building also realized energy savings from reduced transportation needs: Local materials and products manufactured within five hundred miles of San Francisco account for at least 20 percent of all construction materials. The Academy provides secure bicycle parking at its front and back entrances,

BLUE JEANS MAKE GREEN INSULATION

To keep its new building warm, the Academy chose to use insulation made from recycled blue jeans instead of standard fiberglass or foam-based products. With its thick cotton batting, made from post-industrial recycled denim, blue jean insulation offers an organic alternative to formaldehyde-laden insulation materials. It also holds more heat and absorbs sound better than spun fiberglass insulation, and it's safer to handle. Even when denim insulation is treated with fire retardants and fungicides to prevent mildew, it's still easier to work with and doesn't require installers to wear respirators or protective clothes.

The continuous, flat canopy around the roofline creates a calm silhouette that helps the building blend into the park's landscape below the tree line.

ABOVE Brewer's blackbirds perch on beams during construction of the new Academy, whose living roof will provide habitat for native birds and insects in Golden Gate Park.

as well as a recharging station for electric cars, offers a discount to visitors who take public transportation, and provides incentives for staff to walk, bike, or take public transportation to work.

WATER EFFICIENCY Throughout the building, water systems were designed to reduce reliance on municipal supplies of potable water. Low-flow bathroom fixtures regulate water use, consume 20 percent less water than required by code, and contain miniturbines that generate their own power. The building is also plumbed to use recycled water in toilets and to backwash aquarium filters. The new aquarium uses reduced amounts of salt-water piped in through Golden Gate Park from the Pacific Ocean compared to the old Steinhart and employs natural systems to purify nitrate wastes, ensuring that the aquarium water can be recycled.

LIVING ROOF But it's the Academy's colorful, dramatic living roof—a rolling, 2.5-acre expanse of plants and wildflowers—that makes the California Academy of Sciences the world's greenest museum. Its seven hills

rise above the roofline, blanketed with nine species of native California plants, and echo the topography of the park and the green hillsides of San Francisco. It is the largest living roof in California and the most complex living roof ever constructed.

Renzo Piano likes to call it a "flying carpet." His sketch for an undulating living roof that integrated the new facility into Golden Gate Park was "a masterstroke of design," former board chairman Richard Bingham says, that made the park's environment a part of the Academy itself. Piano recalls that he felt inspiration the first time he set foot on the rooftop of the old Academy building. "I was above ground," he says, "but swimming in the middle of trees. I immediately felt that that experience was an essential piece of the new building. The original roof had a cupola covered in red tile on top of the planetarium, which was taller than the rest of the building. My idea of having a roof that goes up and down was part of that observation. Step by step, the roof design became more clear, and a few months later, we began to see that the roof had to be green."

Covered with 1.7 million California plants, the living roof blends with the contours of the landscape and creates the largest undiluted swath of native vegetation in San Francisco. It also creates a new link in the ecological corridor and new habitat for honeybees, hummingbirds, butterflies, and other creatures. To select species of plants for the roof, Academy botanist and research director Frank Almeda worked with a team of architects and living-roof experts. The plants needed to be able to thrive with little water, resist the salt content from the ocean air, and tolerate wind. "Our goal was to choose native plants that would provide much-needed habitat and were well adapted to the climate in Golden Gate Park," Almeda says. "We also needed to select species that would look attractive throughout the year, since a visually appealing roof is a much more powerful educational tool."

After extensive testing with thirty native California species, the roof was planted with nine that will need no artificial irrigation and can self-propagate: beach strawberry *(Fragaria chiloensis)* produces berries that attract

OPPOSITE PAGE TOP Mock-ups of the living roof enabled Rana Creek habitat designers to determine which plants would be best suited to the sloping environment.

BOTTOM Containers of native plants—including self-heal *(Prunella vulgaris)*—bloom on the steep grades of the living roof.

LEFT The living roof's coconut-fiber planting trays will soon biodegrade, leaving a lush carpet of plants and wildflowers.

native birds; self-heal (*Prunella vulgaris*) bears large tubular flowers that attract hummingbirds and bumble-bees; sea pink (*Armeria maritima* ssp. *californica*) produces pom-pom-like flowers favored by moths and butterflies; stonecrop (*Sedum spathulifolium*) produces nectar for the threatened San Bruno elfin butterfly; tidytips (*Layia platy-glossa*) attract wasps and pirate bugs that feed on pest insects; miniature lupine (*Lupinus bicolor*) and California poppies (*Eschscholzia californica*) provide nectar for bees and butterflies; California plantain (*Plantago erecta*) hosts a variety of butterfly larvae; and the bright yellow flowers produced by goldfield plants (*Lasthenia californica*) attract a wide variety of beneficial native insects.

After preparing the approximately 110,000-square-foot rooftop to accommodate this living tapestry of native plant species, the next challenge, Almeda says, was to keep plants and soil from sliding off the roof's extreme dips and slopes. The solution was to use porous trays made from tree sap and coconut husks as containers for the vegetation. These trays line the rooftop like tiles and

enable the roots to grow and spread, stabilizing the soil as the trays themselves biodegrade.

The roof's six-inch bed of soil, he adds, is more than just a planting medium. The soil padding helps reduce low-frequency noise by forty decibels and provides a thermal insulating layer for the building that helps prevent over-heating during the warmest months, keeping interior temperatures about ten degrees cooler than a standard roof would and reducing the need for air-conditioning.

The living roof also curbs the "urban heat island effect." Typical black tar-and-asphalt roofs and pavement trap heat, causing cities to be six to ten degrees warmer than outlying greenbelt areas. The living roof decreases the heat island effect often created by large buildings, staying about forty degrees cooler than a standard roof. Its undulating topography, with slopes up to forty-five degrees, also draws cool air into the open piazza at the building's center, naturally ventilating the surrounding exhibit spaces; skylights in the roof automatically open and close to vent hot air. The photovoltaic cells in the

glass canopy bordering the living roof project out, creating a sheltered, landscaped public green space that shields the building from excessive light, reducing energy consumption and blurring the boundaries between the building and the park around it.

The green roof also helps curb pollution and flooding from storm-water runoff, which carries salt, sand, soil, pesticides, fertilizers, oil, litter, and other pollutants into nearby ecosystems. Most buildings make little or no effort to capture or treat runoff, but the green roof of the new Academy absorbs 98 percent of all storm-water flows, keeping up to two million gallons of runoff per year out of the environment. It also has a filter fabric that helps clean particulates from storm water before it enters the drainage system. Any remaining storm water is channeled underground to recharge chambers for park aquifers that provide recycled water for irrigation.

Although most living roofs offer no public access, an open-air observation terrace enables Academy visitors to get a close-up look at the roof's lush canopy of plants. This

ABOVE FAR LEFT The porous planting trays, made from tree sap and coconut husks, are portable and easy to install.

MIDDLE Young plants grown by Rana Creek fill hundreds of trays in the Carmel Valley.

RIGHT As the plants mature, their roots will grow from one tray into another, knitting together the surface of the living roof.

ABOVE *the* ACADEMY : LIFE *on the* LIVING ROOF

The idea of greening a roof dates back thousands of years. Civilizations in Mesopotamia originated the concept, and sod roofs have long provided warmth and insulation to homes in cold, wet climates like Scandinavia. The green roof concept as we know it today, however, was developed in Germany in the 1960s, and—though the idea is still in its infancy in the United States—green roofs have become increasingly common in the United Kingdom, Switzerland, Austria, and Japan.

The Academy of Sciences' living roof, funded by the Osher Foundation, is more complex than any other and presented challenges. The first task was choosing the right plants. "Green roofs have no equivalent in nature," explains Academy botanist Frank Almeda. "They are engineered, fabricated systems and unusual environments for plant life, so selecting the right plants species was

critical." Green roofs have different microclimates with respect to sun, shade, and wind patterns. Surrounding buildings or trees can create wind tunnels or prevalent periods of shade during the course of a day. The Academy's plant choice was also limited because of the shallow, lightweight planting medium on the roof and the lack of traditional irrigation.

Before the Academy's original home in Golden Gate Park was torn down in 2004, Almeda and his team spent two years testing over thirty species of native plants in full-scale mockups of roof sections. In steeply sloped planter boxes on the roof and in the central courtyard, test plants were left to grow without fertilization or irrigation. "We monitored the species for two years," he says, "looking at growth rate, cover, attractiveness, and how well they responded to the elements." Surviving this trial, nine

(continued on next page . . .)

hardy finalists were chosen: four perennial plants that Almeda affectionately refers to as "The Fabulous Four"—sea pink, beach strawberry, self-heal, and stonecrop—and five annual wildflowers, California poppy, tidytips, miniature lupine, goldfield, and California plantain. These nine species attract a wide variety of native wildlife, including the endangered Bay checkerspot and San Bruno elfin butterflies.

The unusually steep grades of the Academy's roof also created problems with plant installation. To solve them, the architects and SWA landscape designers worked with the nursery that grew plants for the Academy's roof—Rana Creek in Carmel Valley, California—to develop an innovative, sustainable strategy that prevents plants and soil from sliding down steep slopes. Using tree sap and coconut husk fiber, a waste product from coconut plants in the Philippines, they created porous, biodegradable trays, three inches deep and seventeen inches square, for growing the Academy's plants. Fifty thousand of the

coconut husk trays were ultimately installed, like tiles, on the Academy's roof. Within a few weeks, the plants' roots grew from one coconut husk tray into the next, locking the trays together in a tightly woven patchwork quilt of vegetation. The trays will slowly biodegrade over the next several years, leaving a well-established carpet of plants and wildflowers. A wide grid of rock gabions—wire mesh cages filled with rocks—provides additional rigidity and support and creates walkways that facilitate roof maintenance.

As time passes and the roof interacts dynamically with its environment, its appearance and inhabitants will change. "Two to three years out," Almeda says, "we may find that we're learning something new. The living roof is an experiment," he adds, "and it will evolve. But already, native bees and insects are coming to the roof that never came before. Wildlife is finding it."

Skylights above the planetarium allow maximum daylight to penetrate the Coral Reef Tank below the dome.

expansive vista encompasses the densest concentration of native wildflowers in San Francisco and is an ideal location for watching birds, butterflies, and insects.

PLANETARIUM *and* RAINFOREST GLOBES The undulations in the living roof roll above the Academy's groundbreaking new planetarium, rainforest, and aquarium exhibits. The two ninety-foot globes that encase the planetarium and rainforest extend sharply above the roof, creating steep hills and, Renzo Piano says, "a tension between the container and the contained."

Inside the globe that houses the new Morrison Planetarium is a dome that, unlike those in most planetariums, is tilted at a thirty-degree angle, mimicking the tilt of planet Earth and allowing visitors to feel that they are not just looking up at space but are immersed in stars. The dome's tilted frame, composed of 100 percent recycled steel, provides attachment points for plaster and fiberglass panels that form the exterior surface. Inside the steel frame is a NanoSeam projection screen, a new technology that is designed to appear entirely seamless;

although the screen is constructed of separate aluminum panels, the seams between them are engineered to disappear in certain lighting. Tiny perforations across the screen enable audio speakers, ventilation ducts, and other equipment to be situated above and around the outside of the screen, leaving the interior uncluttered. Properly lit, the dome seems infinite to the entering visitor, creating a uniquely realistic astronomical experience in its re-creation of a remote, pristine, and luminous universe. The tilted planetarium dome is cantilevered out over the deepest living-coral display in the world—a 212,000-gallon tank inhabited by delicate soft and hard corals, as well as sharks, rays, and more than four thousand colorful reef fishes.

A second globe, on the opposite side of the building's piazza, contains the Academy's new Rainforests of the World exhibit. This transparent dome, made of double-curved, laminated, superclear glass, measures ninety feet in diameter. Visitors ascend a ramp through the top three floors of the exhibit, experiencing a variety of rainforest environments representing Borneo, Madagascar,

Skylights in the Academy's roof admit as much natural light as possible into the rainforest dome below. Some skylights are operable to increase natural ventilation and temperature control in the exhibit hall.

In the rainforest dome, life-support lighting systems supplement daylight whenever necessary.

and Costa Rica. The spiraling ramp features such complex geometry and tight curves that a roller-coaster manufacturer was hired to shape the steel. An elevator then brings visitors down into the Amazonian Flooded Forest, where they walk through an underwater tunnel that provides views into a hundred-thousand-gallon tank. A special misting system maintains temperatures within the rainforest globe at eighty-two to eighty-five degrees Fahrenheit and at 75 percent humidity or higher. Heat-sensing skylights open like clamshells, automatically, venting the exhibit hall and allowing natural light to reach the plants below. Powerful metal halide lights provide additional growing power.

SETTING *a* GREEN STANDARD From the basement to the roof, the choices behind each element of the new Academy's construction reflect a commitment to energy efficiency, reducing the Academy's carbon footprint, and preserving the natural world. They express, Frank Almeda says, "a way of understanding that Earth can remain our home, but it's not ours alone. If a natural history museum doesn't make that commitment, who will?"

The Academy project has already won international recognition for its commitment to sustainability and green design. In 2005, the building was selected as the North American winner of the silver Holcim Award for Sustainable Construction. The competition, organized by the Holcim Foundation in collaboration with five of the world's leading technical universities, promotes sustainable approaches to the built environment. The new Academy was also awarded the U.S. Environmental Protection Agency's regional 2006 Environmental Award in recognition of its sustainable design, and it is one of ten pilot "green building" projects of the San Francisco Department of the Environment.

The California Academy of Sciences has also been working with the U.S. Green Building Council to earn a Platinum-level LEED (Leadership in Energy and Environmental Design) certificate. Launched in 1998, the LEED program implements nationally recognized guidelines for sustainable design and construction. LEED-certified buildings often cost less to operate and maintain and can produce significantly fewer carbon emissions than conventional buildings do.

Points for the coveted LEED certificate are awarded in five key areas: sustainable site development, water savings, energy efficiency, materials selection, and indoor environmental quality. The U.S. Green Building Council offers four levels of LEED certificates (Certified, Silver, Gold, and Platinum). Midway through the architectural design process, the California Academy of Sciences discovered that its new building already merited the second-highest LEED rating, Gold, and was well on its way to achieving the highest level, Platinum. Design and engineering needed only minimal adjustment—such as adding floor mats and recycled carpeting in some areas—to achieve the highest ranking, at a cost of less than 1 percent of the building's budget. The Academy committed to meeting that challenge. "Our goal," states William Patterson, chairman of the board since 2007, "has been to earn international recognition as the world's largest LEED Platinum-certified public space."

OPPOSITE PAGE The piazza's transparent walls offer views into the rainforest dome, the park, and the exhibit floor.

ABOVE In the Academy's research and administration building, automatic and manually operated windows provide comfort, views, sunlight, and natural ventilation for new office spaces.

LEFT Articulated ball joints serve as structural nodes in the piazza canopy.

EVOLUTIONARY DESIGN The new building, says former board chairman Richard Bingham, embodies the museum's revitalized mission and "crystallizes change" at the Academy. Still, even though its doors are open to the public, the enormously complex building will remain a work in progress for several years. While other facilities have installed passive heating and cooling systems, and other museums have built rainforests or planetariums, none have ever combined all these elements within a single building. Although every element has been tried and tested, the Academy will continue to fine-tune each of them so they work in harmony.

The new building will also become a stage for energizing people and educating them about the world they live in. "The Academy is much more than a building," Frank Almeda says. "It's a vessel for teaching people about biodiversity and how to protect it." The quest for sustainability never overshadowed its other purposes—or, Piano says, the magic of its architectural design.

"For me," Piano confides, "there's magic in the transparency between the building and the park, in the relation between spaces. It is in the piazza, where you feel protected from wind and rain by a very light spider's web. When you walk around on a sunny day, the photovoltaic cells on the edge of the canopy scatter vibrant shadows that look like leaves on the spaces underneath." Those solar cells produce energy, but they also create a kind of subtle beauty in a place, he says, "where the rational and the poetic come together."

Viewed from the Music Concourse, the Academy's landscaping and living roof fulfill Renzo Pianos's ambition to integrate the building almost seamlessly into the surrounding natural environment of Golden Gate Park.

PART 2

EXPLORING, EXPLAINING, PROTECTING

Skylights drench the Rainforests of the World exhibit in natural light.

CH 3 The Academy of Sciences' new building is an architectural wonder, but its purpose is to inspire wonder—at the diversity of life on Earth, at how all of it evolved and can survive. "When a six-year-old touches the spiny arm of a sea star, or when a sixty-year-old fully grasps the meaning of climate change," explains executive director Gregory Farrington," those are the moments, the 'wow' and the 'hmmm,' that the Academy strives for."

But those moments have been harder and harder to come by for natural history museums. Most are hobbled by aging, unchanging exhibits that seem out of step with science, life, and technology in the twenty-first century. Many are also predictable, with generic displays of gemstones and dinosaur bones. The new Academy, by contrast, has charted a distinct course, with exhibits shaped by its singular scientific collections and contributions.

"The California Academy of Sciences has unique stories to tell," Farrington ex-plains—about climate change, California,

evolution, adaptation, and extinction. Those stories, told in dynamic, interactive exhibits, stir the mind and imagination, touching people's emotions, he says, "by taking our scientists' passion and putting it out there on the museum floor."

ACROSS SEA, LAND, *and* SPACE The exhibits are integral elements of the new building. "To design good exhibits," Renzo Piano says, "you have to be a good poet and a good scientist." His group collaborated with Academy staff and exhibit designers to build inventive museum experiences and explorable landscapes that, like the building itself, are transparent: they expose behind-the-scenes research, collections, and operations. "Across sea, land, and space," Farrington says, "they engage and immerse people in the wonders and diversity of life on Earth and the challenge that we're facing to sustain it."

Life, in fact, infuses and animates the museum. The strange and beautiful creatures of the aquarium, once found only in their own hall, now swim and splash in every corner of the building. Dialogue, too, is a concept that drives both the architecture and the exhibit floors; face-to-face interactions with Academy scientists and trained docents personalize and enliven the museum landscape.

It's an open, accessible approach that's rare among natural history museums, adds former executive director Patrick Kociolek. "Many museums speak down to the public," he says. "We wanted to do the opposite, to bring people back." To discover new ways of engaging visitors, the Academy turned to experts beyond the museum world, recruiting retail and branding designers whose clients ranged from Sony and MTV to Anthropologie and Urban Outfitters. Through intensive brainstorming with the Renzo Piano Building Workshop and Academy staff, designers immersed themselves in the mission, science, and architectural vision of the new Academy, creating flexible, interactive, media-rich exhibits that attract and inspire.

the STEINHART AQUARIUM: WATER and LIFE
With a thousand species and four times as many indi-

vidual animals as the Academy's old aquarium, the new Steinhart displays an immense diversity of creatures that live in, over, and under the water. "The new Steinhart Aquarium is not just about fish," says aquarium director Chris Andrews. "It's about water and life and all the mixed communities of life that water sustains."

The new Steinhart combines iconic large-scale habitats, intimate smaller exhibits, and unique displays with elements that will change on a regular basis. It also embodies the Academy's transparent, multilevel approach in its new home. On the museum's ground floor and above, visitors view the large aquarium exhibits as patches of nature in a human-made building. On the Academy's lower level, however, "the architecture falls away," says Tom Hennes, principal of Thinc, the museum, attraction, and aquarium exhibition design firm that planned and designed the Steinhart exhibits. "It's as if people are looking into a natural space full of wonder and mystery," with displays that are geographically specific and naturalistic. "The Academy," he adds, "has a higher responsibility to portray real places and real habitats, because this is a

FOOD *for* THOUGHT

At the new Academy café and restaurant, food is more than a culinary issue—it is edible exhibit programming about the many connections between food and culture.

Run by Loretta Keller and Charles Phan, two of San Francisco's premier chefs, the restaurant also seamlessly integrates the Academy's focus on green approaches. Instead of typical museum fare, like Polish hot dogs and curly fries, it offers sustainable, organic, seasonal food from local suppliers. All ingredients used in the multi-cultural, kid-friendly menu meet the State of California's organic standards, grown by farms that are operated as sustainable enterprises. The restaurant elevates the quality of museum food for a wide demographic, and the variety, preparation, and presentation of its dishes are "curated" as part of an endowed Academy exhibit on the Anthropology of Food.

world-class research institution that studies real places and authoritatively teaches things about the real world." Through up-close interactions with divers, staff, docents, and animals on the public floor, visitors see how creatures are cared for and gain insight into the fundamental challenges animals face in the wild. "The new aquarium," Chris Andrews says, "is all about conveying our passion for the natural world and trying to spark that passion and concern in others."

Not everything in the aquarium has been reinvented. The swamp—popular with generations of Steinhart visitors—is back, complete with bass, catfish, and other southeastern American fishes; snapping turtles; and live alligators, including an albino. Beyond the subtropical swamp, however, the aquarium's landscape has changed radically. Instead of the fish Roundabout and galleries of smaller tanks, the new, expanded Steinhart is composed of four major exhibits—the Philippine Coral Reef, the Water Planet, the California Coast, and Rainforests of the World. Together, these geographically diverse exhibits— enriched with living creatures, hands-on activities, and

multimedia experiences—tell the life story of water: its properties, habitats, and necessity to all life on Earth. "Water connects everything," Andrews says—and in the new Steinhart, there's more water everywhere.

the PHILIPPINE CORAL REEF A 212,000-gallon tank, twenty-five feet in depth, holds the world's deepest living-coral-reef display—a feature so large that it forms part of the structural support for the Academy building. One hundred twenty metal halide lamps, originally designed to flood sports stadiums with light, supplement and simulate the intensity and spectrum of natural sunlight to sustain the living corals, which are difficult to grow at depths greater than six feet.

Most people have never seen a living reef. Often called rainforests of the sea, coral reefs are among the most diverse—and most endangered—aquatic ecosystems on Earth. Up to 70 percent of the world's tropical coral reefs may disappear within fifteen years as a result of global warming and other environmental stressors. More than 25 percent have already been destroyed or badly damaged,

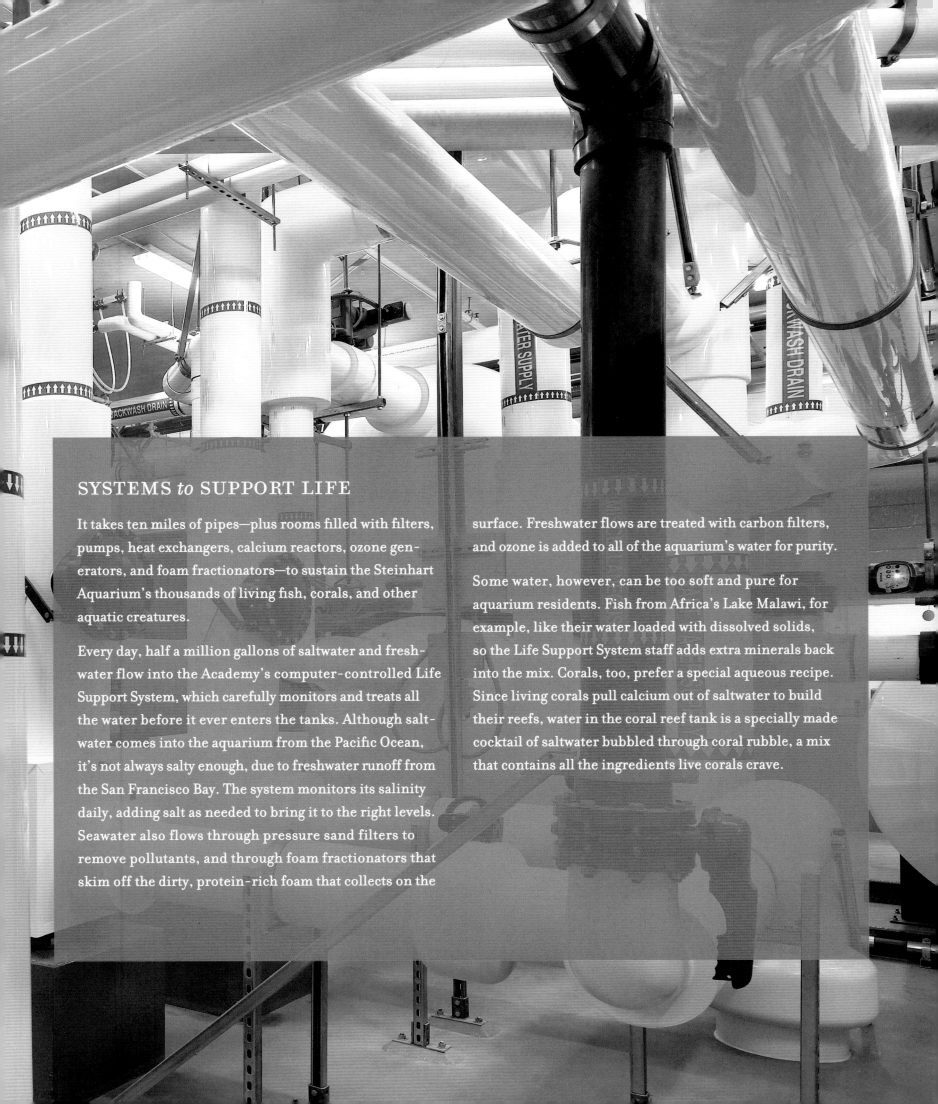

SYSTEMS *to* SUPPORT LIFE

It takes ten miles of pipes—plus rooms filled with filters, pumps, heat exchangers, calcium reactors, ozone generators, and foam fractionators—to sustain the Steinhart Aquarium's thousands of living fish, corals, and other aquatic creatures.

Every day, half a million gallons of saltwater and freshwater flow into the Academy's computer-controlled Life Support System, which carefully monitors and treats all the water before it ever enters the tanks. Although saltwater comes into the aquarium from the Pacific Ocean, it's not always salty enough, due to freshwater runoff from the San Francisco Bay. The system monitors its salinity daily, adding salt as needed to bring it to the right levels. Seawater also flows through pressure sand filters to remove pollutants, and through foam fractionators that skim off the dirty, protein-rich foam that collects on the surface. Freshwater flows are treated with carbon filters, and ozone is added to all of the aquarium's water for purity.

Some water, however, can be too soft and pure for aquarium residents. Fish from Africa's Lake Malawi, for example, like their water loaded with dissolved solids, so the Life Support System staff adds extra minerals back into the mix. Corals, too, prefer a special aqueous recipe. Since living corals pull calcium out of saltwater to build their reefs, water in the coral reef tank is a specially made cocktail of saltwater bubbled through coral rubble, a mix that contains all the ingredients live corals crave.

and the ones that remain are important to preserve because of the biodiversity they contain, the coastal protection they offer against tropical storms, and the food and livelihood they provide for millions of people.

Coral reefs in the Philippines are among the most biodiverse reef systems in the world, and they are a prime research focus for Academy scientists. At the new Steinhart, divers equipped with communication gear explain the reef's inner workings as visitors explore slopes and caves filled with thousands of corals and reef fishes, as well as a Philippine mangrove habitat and reef lagoon. Mangrove habitats are vital but endangered nurseries for sharks, turtles, shrimp, small crabs, juvenile pipefish, and other animals and small fishes that live in and around mangrove roots. Scientists at the Academy and in the Philippines have been collaborating to document the rich biodiversity of the Philippine reefs and to develop strategies that will help preserve these habitats, whether by creating marine parks or by supporting sustainable fisheries in the future.

the CALIFORNIA COAST Shaped by waves and tides, the rocky coast of Northern California contains some of the world's richest temperate marine habitats, in proximity to eight million inhabitants of the San Francisco Bay Area. Since its creation in 1981, the Gulf of the Farallones National Marine Sanctuary, outside San Francisco Bay, has led to the return to these waters of several great whale species and the recovery of several other endangered marine mammals—a compelling conservation success story. The California Coast exhibit's hundred-thousand-gallon tank and smaller focus tanks teem with fish, small sharks, abalone, and sea urchins and bring a bit of the Farallones sanctuary to the city. Hands-on interactions with living algae, sea stars, and crabs in a tide-pool habitat help visitors understand how organisms survive in high-energy wave environments.

Nearby, a Southern California tank provides comparison and contrast, showing how marine life is lived along the state's southern coast. With climate change and ocean warming, some Southern California species, such

The one-hundred-thousand-gallon California Coast tank features the rich, diverse marine habitats of the Gulf of the Farallones National Marine Sanctuary.

This *Echinopora* species is one of many live corals in the Philippine Coral Reef exhibit, most of them cultured through sustainable methods.

as brightly colored Garibaldi fish, may soon be seen farther north.

A Giants Tank displays giant sea bass and moray eels, and a giant Pacific octopus tank features the world's largest species of octopus. Commonly found off the Northern California coast, the giant Pacific octopus is one of the world's most intelligent invertebrates. It likes stimulation and can learn through observation, and visitors watch its playful and educational interactions with staff biologists.

the WATER PLANET The heart of the new Steinhart Aquarium is the Water Planet—a luminous exhibit hosting a wide range of interactive sensory experiences explaining, as never before, the link between aquatic habitats and life on land. As visitors descend into the Water Planet environment, they are surrounded by iridescent fiberglass walls designed to capture a sense of liquid flow, created with the help of software usually used for modeling airplanes and automobiles. Within the watery space, four exhibit "islands" demonstrate how

sea horses, snakes, frogs, fish, and other animals move, sense, reproduce, and adapt to life in arid environments and in water in its many forms—from fresh to salt and from warm to cold. Once an hour or so, a multimedia display fills the undulating walls with images of aquatic life, turning them into an immersive theater-in-the-round exploring water as the essence of all life on Earth.

RAINFORESTS *of the* WORLD A major iconic element of the reinvented Steinhart Aquarium is the new Rainforests of the World exhibit. Encased in a transparent, ninety-foot-diameter glass globe designed by Renzo Piano, it is the first spherical living rainforest display in the United States. In no other exhibit can visitors explore the three-dimensional aspect of tropical rainforests—which are incredibly rich, diverse, and severely threatened—and the unique qualities of different rainforests around the world. Surrounded by some sixteen hundred living Amazonian fishes, Borneo fruit bats, carnivorous pitcher plants, Malagasy chameleons, and Costa Rican butterflies, visitors ascend from a Borneo

forest floor through a Malagasy understory to a Costa Rican canopy in a humid living rainforest that soars sixty feet up.

The dome is split vertically into two sections. Half houses a living neotropical rainforest that spans all four floors of the exhibit, from the underwater flooded forest to the treetop canopy. The other half houses four galleries filled with hundreds of rainforest inhabitants from the Amazon Basin, Borneo, Madagascar, and Costa Rica. A pathway spirals up through the exhibit, passing through three different galleries, vertical zones, and geographic locations. The Borneo gallery features a large cave filled with bats, bat-eating snakes, and invertebrates, while a path lined with live orchids and carnivorous pitcher plants leads to exhibits with flying frogs, flying snakes, and flying lizards. The Madagascar gallery explores why some 80 percent of that island's animals—including more than half the world's species of chameleons—exist only on Madagascar, and why their survival is threatened. More than 90 percent of Madagascar's natural wildlife habitat has been destroyed, and Academy

FAR LEFT TOP Skylights, reflected in the water of the Rainforests of the World exhibit, draw natural light below the surface of the flooded Amazon forest.

FAR LEFT BOTTOM Half the chameleon species in the world, including this panther chameleon, *Furcifer pardalis,* live in the tropical forests of Madagascar. This one may also be found in the understory of the Academy's rainforest exhibit.

BOTTOM CENTER A study model shows the view upward through the rainforest globe.

LEFT Natural light streams through superclear glass that encases the Rainforests of the World exhibit.

researchers have been working closely with Malagasy scientists to identify and protect its endangered species. In the Costa Rican gallery, more than fifteen species of free-flying birds and colorful longwing butterflies wheel through the bright, airy canopy layer, which represents the habitat of some 90 percent of rainforest species. In this gallery, visitors encounter a message of hope, since Costa Rica has committed itself to rainforest conservation efforts, ecotourism, and sustainable land use.

A glass elevator then carries visitors down to the Amazonian Flooded Forest, where they get a fish-eye view of the submerged world of the forest floor. During the rainy season in the Amazon River Basin, floodwaters rise forty to sixty feet. Fish and freshwater dolphins move into the rainforest with the rising waters, while many ground-dwelling species such as jaguar travel to higher ground. As visitors approach an underwater tunnel, water levels in the tanks reveal increasingly submerged habitats, tracing the progress of a rainforest flood, while hundreds of fish—including giant catfish, silver arowanas, spotted peacock bass, and vegetarian piranhas—cruise overhead. A live anaconda shares this gallery, where interactive exhibits allow visitors to feel the jolt from an electric eel and the constricting, predatory power of an anaconda. On their journey through the Rainforests of the World exhibit, visitors experience a full spectrum of life in the world's most diverse and most threatened terrestrial ecosystems.

PLANETARIUM DOME On the opposite side of the building's central piazza, a matching ninety-foot dome houses the Academy's new Morrison Planetarium. Its screen, seventy-five feet in diameter, forms the largest fully digital dome in the world, and its new projection and software technologies produce the most accurate interactive digital universe ever created. "The new Morrison allows us to explore space more deeply and differently than ever before," explains Ryan Wyatt, who directs the planetarium and heads science visualization for the Academy. In the original planetarium, all the seats faced toward the center, "like a campfire under the night sky," Wyatt explains. The new Morrison has a unidirectional orientation, with seats facing forward in a dome tilted

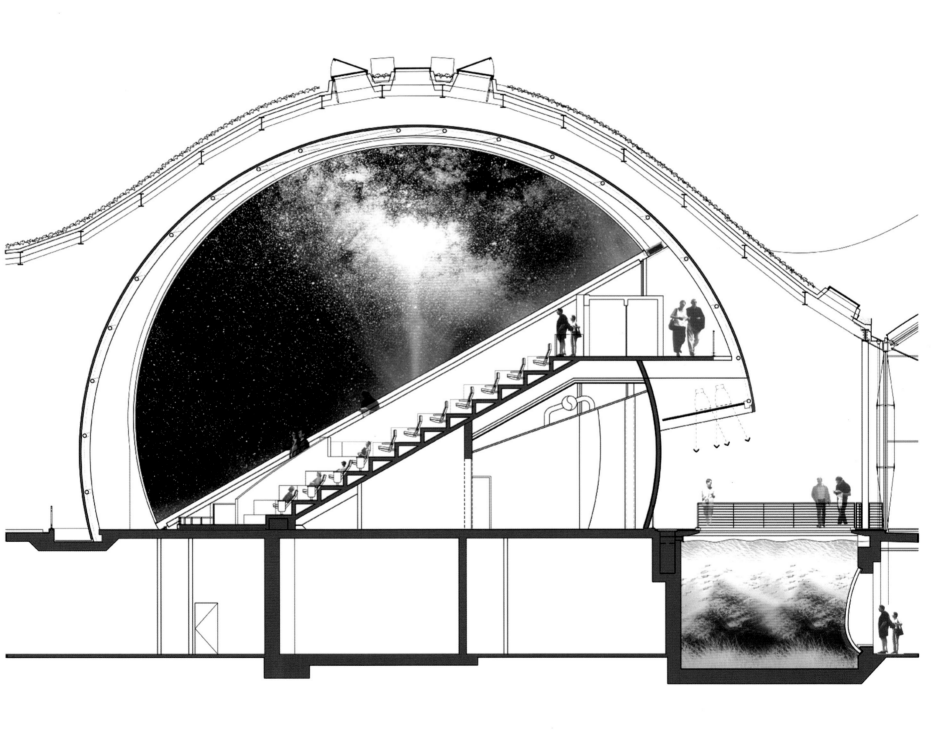

at thirty degrees. The result is a powerful experience: "Individuals collectively fly through the universe," Wyatt says. The audience becomes part of the action and part of the science. Live NASA feeds take visitors on trips through outer space, and computer-generated visuals, based on astronomical data, vividly depict new discoveries.

The new Morrison, Wyatt adds, expands the traditional role of planetariums, moving beyond astronomy to explore and explain the evolution and sustainability of life on our home planet. "We connect closely with research at the Academy," he explains—transporting visitors to remote places on Earth, where Academy scientists are working, and showing how climate change is altering the distribution of species on the planet. "It's a fundamental shift in the way people think of planetariums and where technology can take us."

KIMBALL NATURAL HISTORY MUSEUM Beyond the aquarium, rainforest, and planetarium, the California Academy of Sciences is a natural history museum—one that has been reinvented as a multisensory showcase

for the Academy's own research and collections. It still retains links to the past, however. The new Kimball Natural History Museum—named for former board chairman William Kimball—features the Tusher African Center, a re-creation and update of African Hall, which had been one of San Francisco's best-loved attractions since it opened in the 1930s. Its diorama animals, some of them eighty years old, were cleaned and repaired, and many of the hall's features—its dimensions, scenic paintings, bronze frames, and architectural details—look nearly identical to the originals. But there are new elements, too. Plasma touch screens near dioramas take visitors on virtual safaris through video footage of animals in the wild, and a large, open diorama features a virtual herd of elephants crossing an African savannah. Four dioramas now feature live animals—chameleons, tortoises, a monitor lizard, and endangered cichlids from Lake Malawi. And at the end of African Hall, a new fourteen-foot-high tank showcases a colony of black-footed penguins from the Cape Floristic Region of South Africa, visible above and below

LEFT Favorite dioramas of African Hall
have been re-created and enhanced in the
new Academy with live animals, videos,
and special effects.

the waterline as they dive and gracefully "fly" below the surface.

Designed and produced by Cinnabar, an exhibit production firm with roots in media, retail, and entertainment, the Kimball also brings back another well-loved feature of the old museum: the Foucault pendulum, built in the Academy's own workshops. Swinging continuously in a graceful arc at the end of a thirty-foot-long steel aircraft cable, the pendulum proves, as it has for nearly fifty years, that the Earth rotates on its axis.

New exhibits on California, climate change, and the Academy's own research expeditions fill the rest of the expansive, light-filled museum, which occupies ten thousand square feet of open space surrounding the rainforest and planetarium domes. Accessible from many directions, naturally ventilated, and flooded with daylight, these areas at first presented unusual exhibit-design challenges—partly because, in keeping with the building's green design, the Academy wants them to be flexible and easily changed, reorganized, and reused.

The solution, developed in collaboration with the Renzo Piano Building Workshop, is a "kit of parts," a reusable system for creating displays and exhibits in open spaces. "Everything is light, hanging from the ceiling or growing from the floor, on a grid related to the building," Piano explains. Neutral standardized elements—including steel cables and tubes, wood tables and pedestals, and glass or Plexiglas cases—create the skeleton of each exhibit and can be used over and over again. "The system is like musical paper," Piano says, "and has zero gravity," maintaining a feeling of dynamic transparency throughout the museum floor.

CALIFORNIA, CLIMATE CHANGE, *and* EXPEDITIONS
The Kimball's new exhibits are rooted in the Academy's research and dedicated to the mission of exploring, explaining, and protecting the natural world. The California and Climate Change wing highlights the importance of California as one of the world's biodiversity hot spots, home to many endangered species that are found nowhere else. The exhibit displays specimens from the

The Academy's colony of eighteen black-footed penguins, native to southern Africa, have found a new home at the far end of African Hall.

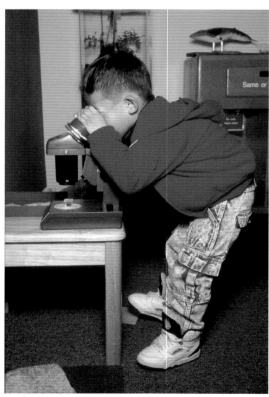

OPPOSITE PAGE TOP Academy educator Jack Laws teaches youngsters about the ecosystem of San Francisco's Mountain Lake.

BOTTOM LEFT With its Early Childhood and Naturalist centers, the Academy is aiming to inspire the next generation of natural scientists.

BOTTOM RIGHT The Academy's architects and designers created a flexible, reusable "kit of parts" for creating displays and exhibits in open spaces.

Academy's unmatched collection of California plants, animals, fossils, and minerals. It also uses California as a case study to explore climate change: the science behind it, its local effects, and steps that can mitigate its drastic results.

The Expeditions gallery, across the piazza, highlights the Academy's past and present research around the world, inviting visitors to practice field research techniques, view specimens from remote and exotic locations, and follow in the footsteps of scientists as they discover new species, adaptations, and evolutionary links. Within this gallery, the Academy's newsroom, Science in Action, presents the latest scientific discoveries, from climate change to the creation of new stars at the far reaches of space. On four flat-screen monitors, the newsroom broadcasts science headlines, fast-breaking news from the world of science, and live talks. The newsroom also presents audio-visual displays, computer stations, and podcasts.

a PLACE *for* LEARNING Education is a core mission of the Academy, Gregory Farrington says, and the new building features new tools and spaces for engaging and inspiring learners of every age. Staffed by education and information specialists and stocked with reference materials, collection samples, and a circulating collection of books and DVDs, the Naturalist Center is a place where students and others can research for school reports; identify their own rocks, leaves, feathers, and other specimens; and learn about environmental sustainability. With its adjoining lab and classrooms, as well as educational programs, it's a resource center for schools and a notable destination for anyone seeking to delve deeper into the workings of the natural world.

Geared toward younger learners, the Early Childhood Center actively introduces preschoolers to natural history. In a fifteen-foot replica of the Academy's 1905 research schooner, the *Academy,* children can imagine life on a sea-based expedition. As young "researchers-in-training" they can compare, sort, and study toddler-

on the NATURE *of* ART

Two art installations—on opposite east and west terraces of the Academy—invite and inspire contemplation about the natural world. Created by artist Maya Lin, who is trained in both art and architecture, the works merge art and science, drawing on the Academy's mission and the building's design.

They were also inspired, in part, by Lin's childhood experience of wonder at the Academy of Sciences. As a fourth-grader, she moved with her family for a year from Ohio to Northern California. "My brother and I went with a neighbor to the Academy in San Francisco. I remember putting my hand in a fish tank and touching an anemone. I also saw the wingspan of a California condor," she says, "and was shocked by its size." Throughout her life, Lin has been committed to wildlife preservation and environmental protection, and her work has long been informed by nature and the natural sciences.

Vaulted to fame by her design for the Vietnam Veterans Memorial in Washington, D.C., Lin has created two spare, powerful pieces for the Academy—her first in the city of San Francisco. On the western exterior terrace of the building, a stainless steel wire landscape "sees" the terrain above and below the water level of the bay. On the opposite terrace, the second installation, entitled "Missing," focuses on extinct and endangered species and places and the loss of biodiversity on the planet. Together, they explore beauty, nature, science, and conservation in two thoughtful works.

friendly research specimens, tend a miniature organic garden, play with plush animals, and explore the world under the soil and under the sea through toys, puzzles, props, costumes, and books.

With its after-school and weekend programs and student internships, the Academy is also working to inspire the next generation of natural scientists. Professional-development resources help teachers increase students' science literacy, and the Academy's career ladder program prepares underrepresented youth for careers in scientific research, education, and administration.

"Sustainability," Farrington says, "is about protecting the life-forms and natural resources of Earth, but it's also about sustaining the vast amount of scientific work that still needs to be done. We can't protect life if we know nothing about it, and we need to mentor and develop a new generation to carry on." But today, he adds, "kids are further and further removed from the natural world—by computer and video games or by where they live."

With its green building, living roof, Steinhart Aquarium, natural history museum, rainforest, planetarium, flexible exhibits, and rich education programs, the Academy is a place, Farrington says, "where kids can get up close and personal with living creatures and discover that there's a real, astonishing natural world out there. It's about reality, surprise and inspiration," a place to build minds and change minds about the wonders, importance, and fragility of the natural world.

At the top of the ninety-foot-high Rainforests of the World exhibit, birds and butterflies fly freely among the branches of the soaring Costa Rican canopy.

Beneath the rainforests, a transparent tunnel guides visitors through a flooded Amazonian forest, where arapaima, giant catfish, and schooling piranhas and tetras swim among submerged roots.

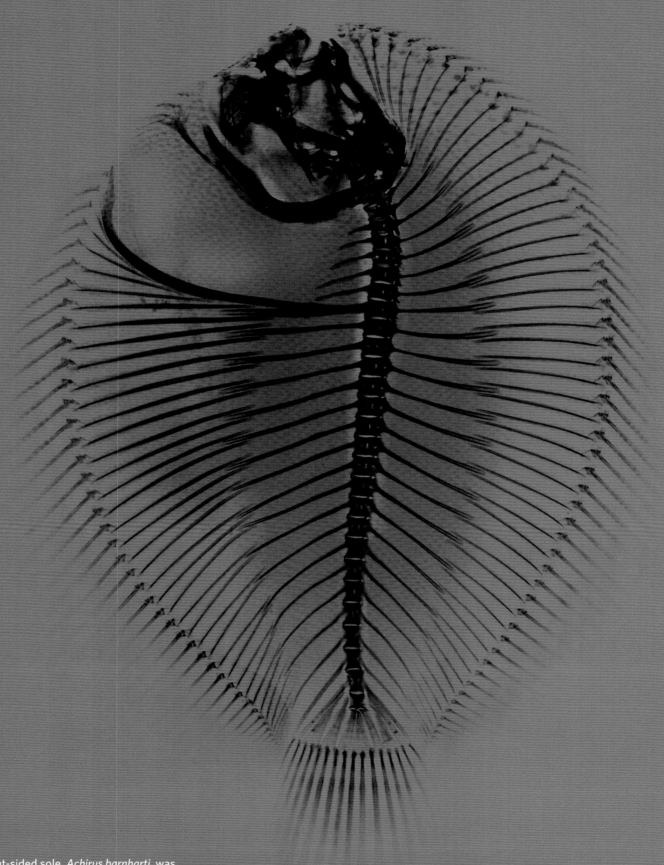

This right-sided sole, *Achirus barnharti,* was caught off Mexico's Coronado Islands in 1923. Its prickly spines and scales account for its common name, hogchoker. These sole live in shallow coastal areas and feed on inverte-brates and small fishes.

CH 4 In the dictionary of life, nouns are all the animals, plants, insects, and living things that inhabit Earth. Today, researchers have discovered that there are many more nouns—most of them still unknown to science—than they ever imagined. "In the 1970s," explains senior scientist and aquatic biology chair John McCosker, "we thought there were as many as ten million living species, and scientists had given seven hundred thousand of them names. Now," he says, "we've identified two million species— but we've learned that there may be a hundred million more that we don't even know about. The world has many more species than we ever realized, and they're disappearing faster than we can discover them."

DISCOVERING LIFE Finding, class- ifying, and naming these new living species before they vanish is a mission of the California Academy of Sciences. Along with the Smithsonian Institution, the natural history museums of London and Paris, Chicago's Field Museum, and the American Museum of Natural History, in New York, the Academy is one of the

ABOVE Many of the Academy's specimens—including fish, reptiles, amphibians, and invertebrates—are preserved in jars of ethanol so that their soft tissues do not deteriorate.

RIGHT New compactors in the Academy's research areas provide 360,000 cubic feet of storage for botanical collections and millions of other specimens.

few remaining institutions in the world to do this work. The Academy's thirty Ph.D. scientists, one hundred research and field assistants, and more than three hundred fellows travel all over the world—to China, Myanmar, New Guinea, and other isolated, often dangerous, biodiversity hot spots—to discover new species of life that have never been seen. Then, with the help of collection managers, curatorial assistants, and graduate students in the various research departments, they spend years studying, classifying, understanding, and naming their specimens—their new, precise "nouns"—so that other scientists can, in McCosker's words, "come up with the verbs, adjectives, and adverbs" of their biology.

However, the Academy's goal is not just to explore and explain life, but also to protect it. "In the face of climate change, understanding Earth's biodiversity is increasingly urgent," says executive director Gregory Farrington. "We can't be effective at protecting any plant or animal if we don't understand it, much less if we don't know it exists." Over the last decade, that urgency has spurred

a new collaborative research approach. Increasingly, Academy scientists from different disciplines have been joining together on expeditions around the globe, pooling their specialized knowledge to establish a baseline of known life on Earth and track the adaptation—or extinction—of many species. Collaboration takes place in the Academy building, too, as scientists combine their data to determine species' ranges, environmental pollutants, and evolutionary pathways, as well as climate change patterns affecting them over time.

BUILDING "COLLABORATORIES" The inefficient layout of the old Academy worked against these kinds of efforts. Departments were isolated from one another, often in separate buildings, and sometimes far removed from the scientific specimen collections they worked with daily. In the new building, Patrick Kociolek says, "we wanted to facilitate multidisciplinary work, to create 'collaboratories' where communities of scientists could easily gather around maps or come together over a cup of coffee." With this goal in mind, the new building's architects literally and metaphorically knocked down walls between different departments. Well-located laboratories, research stations, and break rooms in central areas around the research facility, at the rear of the building, have created a more comfortable, communicative, collaborative research culture for Academy scientists.

The new building also blends research more directly into the visitor experience. "In similar institutions," explains Kociolek, "scientists are almost totally separated from the public. Their research areas have signs warning, 'I'd turn back if I were you.'" The Academy wanted to make its research much more physically and intellectually accessible—transparent to visitors, rather than hidden away. "No museum has ever succeeded in getting the public to understand what research is, why it's important and how it's done," Kociolek says. "But we wanted to do it."

In the new Academy, a project lab on the public floor encourages encounters and exchanges with working scientists. Windows into the laboratory give visitors a view of scientists revealing, sorting, and classifying specimens from recent Academy expeditions. Through video microscopes, they can even see what the scientists are seeing, and docents and interns bring physical specimens out for closer inspection. Multimedia tools take visitors on virtual expeditions, while scientists describe, in their own words, their passion and excitement about their work. "We want the California Academy to be known as the institution where you can come and engage with real scientists in casual, compelling, and real ways," Farrington says; "where scientists can act as mentors and role models for kids and start the next generation of researchers on its way."

a LIBRARY of LIFE The Academy's collection of "nouns"—now numbering twenty million specimens, from microscopic diatoms to jars of New Guinea nudibranchs and preserved whales—is part of the permanent reference archive of life on Earth, the most authoritative and continuous record that science has. The Academy's vast collections, dating back more than a century,

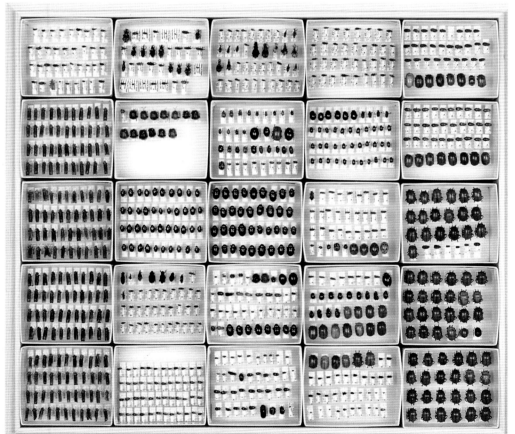

OPPOSITE PAGE Labels on these hummingbird specimens tell when and fairly precisely where they were collected.

TOP LEFT Two frogs preserved in ethanol are among more than five million specimens stored in jars at the Academy. Their bones and cartilage are stained with alcian blue and alizarin blue solutions.

TOP RIGHT This Hopi eagle doll, part of the extensive Elkus Collection, is one of many Native American artifacts belonging to the Anthropology Department.

LEFT This drawer of assorted beetles—weevils, scarabs, and carabids—is part of the Entomology Department's collection of more than twelve million insect and arachnid specimens.

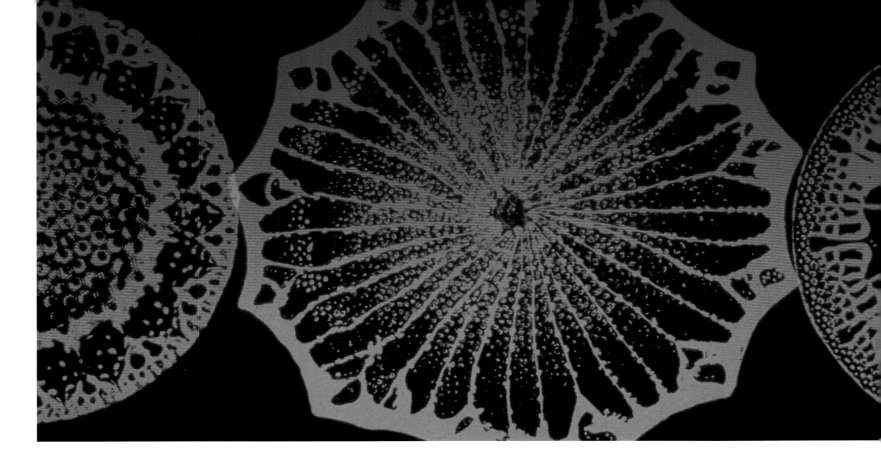

constitute an invaluable research tool for scientists around the world and preserve some of the only genetic and anatomical information that remains about many extinct species. Several of the Academy's specimens, such as the elephant bird and the Falkland Islands fox, are now extinct, and the number of vanishing species is rapidly growing. "We're living during a major episode of mass extinction," explains Peter Roopnarine, the Academy's associate curator of invertebrate zoology and geology. In some cases, the Academy's specimens provide the only evidence that a particular species of life on the planet ever existed.

The Academy's research departments—Anthropology, Aquatic Biology, Botany, Entomology, Herpetology, Ichthyology, Invertebrate Zoology and Geology, and Ornithology and Mammalogy—maintain and develop their own growing collections. The Botany Department manages the sixth-largest herbarium in the United States, with the largest collection of vascular plants in the western states. The Entomology Department is one of the five largest in North America. The Department

of Ornithology and Mammalogy houses the largest collection of marine mammals in the world. The Herpetology Department numbers among the world's top five collections in both size and diversity, and the Ichthyology Department collection, one of the largest fish collections on Earth, houses approximately 50 percent of all fish species known to science. "Each collection," Farrington says, "is a unique and vital resource that documents the diversity of life across place and time."

Storing these priceless specimens is a challenging task. Different types of specimens require different conservation and storage facilities, and in the old Academy, conditions were antiquated and inefficient. Collections were distributed all over the buildings, in basement corners and century-old cabinets that offered little protection from insects and moisture. In the new building, collections are housed in special structures with concrete walls sixteen to eighteen inches thick and precisely controlled humidity, light, and temperature. For wet collections, stored in flammable alcohol, the Academy installed an extensively tested fire-containment system

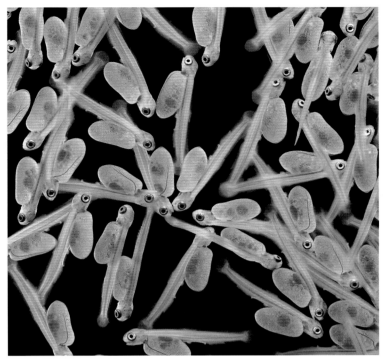

using atomized water, a highly effective nonchemical smothering system used on oil tankers. All the collections are now stored in new state-of-the-art, high-density, compactible storage cabinets that take up some 360,000 cubic feet—equivalent to a ten-foot-wide by nine-foot-high strip of cabinets stretching more than thirteen football fields in length.

CENTER *for* COMPARATIVE GENOMICS In addition to its library of life, the new Academy houses the groundbreaking Center for Comparative Genomics, where scientists can apply the latest technologies, derived from the Human Genome Project, to the field of evolutionary biology. By sequencing and comparing the DNA of plants, animals, and other organisms, scientists can better understand the diversity and evolutionary relationships of life on Earth. The result is akin to a family tree, growing in complexity based on discoveries of the similarity of sequences and anatomical features among organisms. This type of research, known as phylogenetics, forms the core of the behind-the-scenes work at the

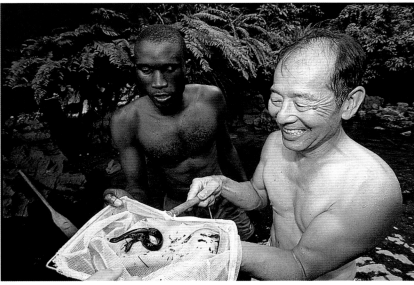

OPPOSITE PAGE Aquatic biologist John McCosker prepares to enter the deep-sea submersible Johnson SeaLink before descending three thousand feet to explore sea life around the Galápagos Islands.

TOP Botanists Peter Fritsch and Bruce Bartholomew gather specimens in the Gaoligong Mountains of southwest China during a monsoon.

ABOVE LEFT The late ornithologist Luis Baptista searches for white-crowned sparrows in Golden Gate Park. Baptista recognized all the individual local white-crowned sparrows by their songs and could often tell where they were born.

ABOVE RIGHT Ichthyologist Tomio Iwamoto admires a freshwater goby caught on the African island of São Tome.

Academy. In the past, biologists used a handful of genes as a proxy for an entire organism. Breakthroughs in genomics, however, have made it possible to look at an organism's entire DNA sequence, or genome, propelling phylogenetics to the next level.

GLOBAL EXPEDITIONS For more than a century— since its schooner *Academy* first voyaged to the Galápagos, in 1905—the California Academy of Sciences has launched expeditions around the world, exploring geographic areas whose ecosystems and plants, animals, and insects are little known. Today, Academy scholars continue to roam the world, focusing on hot spots where many life-forms are under serious threat, to gather information about new species and their fragile environments. Many expeditions are now interdisciplinary projects conducted in partnership with government and conservation agencies. They not only document biodiversity in these ecological hot spots, but also provide advanced training to students and scientists who live there, enabling local specialists to carry on the research and help plan for the conservation of their countries' spectacular rare and threatened ecosystems.

CALIFORNIA ACADEMY *of* SCIENCES RECENT *and* CURRENT EXPEDITIONS

1 MADAGASCAR

Isolated for more than 160 million years, Madagascar contains nearly thirteen thousand unique species of plants and vertebrate animals, many belonging to ancient groups that are now extinct on the mainland. In 2007, the Academy worked with the Malagasy government to found the Madagascar Biodiversity Center, which trains biologists, inventories species, and helps plan conservation strategies. Recent expeditions, focused on arthropods, have discovered eight hundred new species of ants.

2 GALÁPAGOS

Since its first expedition to the Galápagos Islands in 1905, the Academy has been the world's leading center for scientists studying the evolution of Galápagos birds, tortoises, plants, and insects. Recent expeditions, conducted with the government of Ecuador, have studied nudibranch mollusks and resulted in the discovery of thirty new species of marine animals.

3 THE PHILIPPINES

For forty years, the Academy has conducted research in the Philippines, resulting in the discovery of dozens of new animal species. For the last fifteen years, expeditions have explored the biodiversity of coral reef habitats. Academy researchers are working with the country's Bureau of Fisheries and Aquatic Resources to train scientists and are collaborating with Filipino educators and conservation biologists on plans for the long-term preservation of the coral reefs.

4 TANZANIA

In 2006, an Academy expedition traveled to the rainforests of the isolated Udzungwa Mountains in Tanzania with a team of collaborators. The expedition confirmed the existence of a new species of giant elephant shrew—the first such species discovered in 127 years.

5 NAMIBIA

In 2007, Academy scientists traveled to the Namibian desert to trace the evolutionary trajectory of elephant shrew species that have lived in isolation for millions of years. Researchers are using genetics to determine the boundaries of the species' ranges, which will provide clues to understanding evolutionary patterns on the African continent.

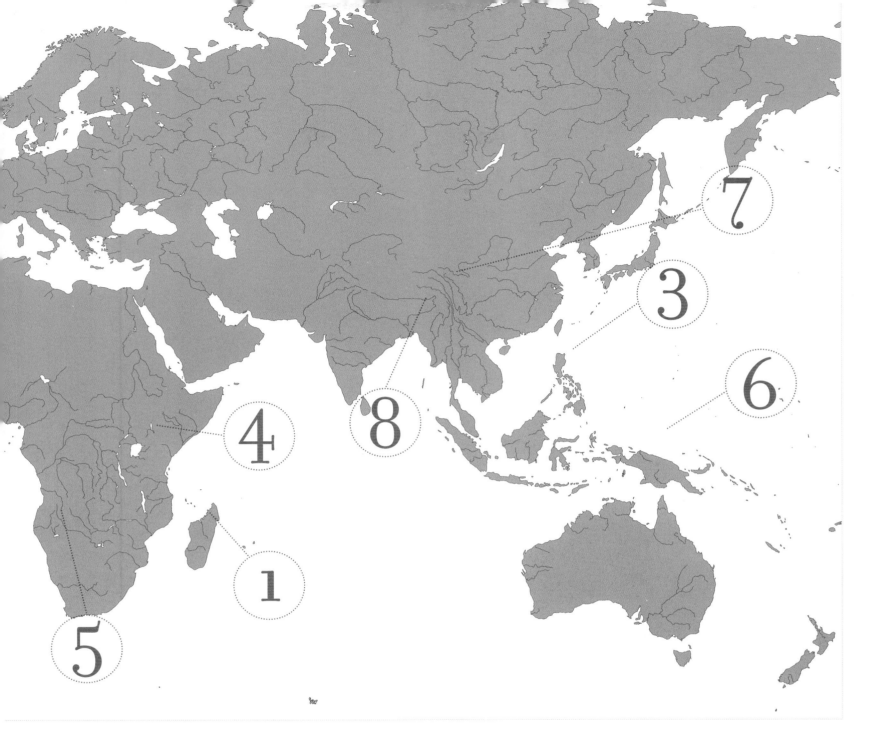

6 NEW GUINEA

Since 1986, Academy scientists from almost all research departments have surveyed birds, plants, insects, and marine animals in New Guinea, discovering more than two hundred new species of nudibranchs and soft corals. Researchers are also documenting how toxicity and bright coloration evolve in birds, how species form, and how populations diverge.

7 YUNNAN, CHINA

In 1998, the Academy launched the China Natural History Project as part of a global collaborative effort to preserve biodiversity in China. Academy botanists, ichthyologists, herpetologists, and mammalogists conducted a biodiversity survey of the isolated Gaoligongshan region of northwestern Yunnan Province, then returned in 2000 and 2002 to undertake further biodiversity survey work with Chinese colleagues.

8 MYANMAR

In 1999, the National Science Foundation funded a three-year collaboration between the California Academy of Sciences, the Smithsonian Institution, and the Nature and Wildlife Conservation Division of Myanmar's Forestry Department to inventory the country's amphibian and reptile species. It was the first systematic herpetological survey ever conducted in the country and helped train Myanmar scientists in systematics, herpetology, conservation biology, and biodiversity research and classification techniques.

9 THE GULF OF GUINEA

Beginning in 1998, the Academy undertook the largest interdisciplinary expeditions in its history to survey the Gulf of Guinea Islands. Four expedition teams have traveled to Bioko, São Tomé, and Príncipe—three volcanic equatorial islands off the west coast of Africa—to document their rich, largely unstudied biodiversity. The surveys of fauna and flora will help determine how small, isolated populations of island species evolved.

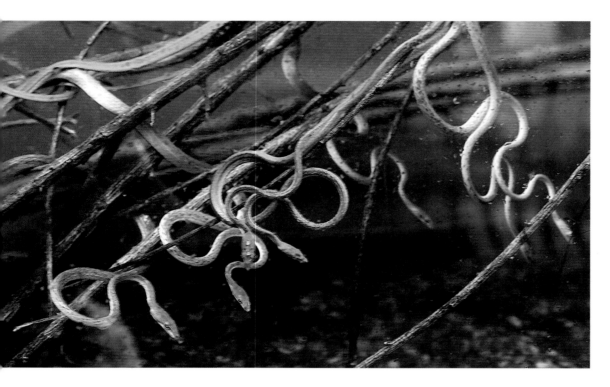

MAPPING BIODIVERSITY Academy researchers have been concerned with global and localized biodiversity since long before the term was coined. Now, says research director Frank Almeda, the Academy is bringing together the expertise of many individuals, along with the resources of several institutions, to answer important questions about biodiversity and conservation. "Conservation, in fact, is becoming more of a centerpiece of our mission," Almeda says, "and the responses of the natural world to climate change will underlie many of our future conservation efforts."

As climates change, habitats change, which has enormous implications for every species on the planet, including humans. Climate change alters temperature and rainfall patterns, shifting the locations where species can survive, and affects all strands of the natural world— the vast array of plant, animal, and microbial life and the network of forests, deserts, coral reefs, tundra, lakes, and oceans. Under these circumstances, a species has three options: it can adapt in place, move as its habitat shifts, or go extinct. A new focus of the Academy's

research is predicting the future distribution of representative plant and animal species in North America as their habitats shift under different climate change scenarios. "By building predictive models," explains Healy Hamilton, head of the Academy's Center for Biodiversity Research and Information, "we can help conservation organizations plan migration corridors among existing protected areas, enabling animals to shift their ranges as climate changes."

The key data researchers use for this sort of planning originates in specimen collections like those in the Academy of Sciences. Collections record the location where each specimen was found, enabling Hamilton and her team to determine baseline data about elevation and ranges of temperature and precipitation for each species habitat. By pooling the environmental parameters of all known localities, the researchers can pinpoint where species are currently known to occur. Then they can alter temperature and precipitation values to reflect the predictions of global climate change models and see where species habitats will occur under different

climate change scenarios. "So much can be done once species' locations are converted to digital dots on maps," Hamilton says. "We can now integrate our bio-diversity information with geographic data and apply it to conservation. We can use specimens in natural history collections to map baseline temperature and precipitation envelopes for a given species, then perturb them by predictions for climate change, and see where new habitats might be."

These efforts, executive director Farrington says, are breathing new life into natural history museum collections, which provide the most verifiable record of life on Earth. "They are also opening a new chapter in the Academy's history of innovation and furthering our mission," he adds, "which is as much about supporting life as it is about documenting its existence."

Academy scientists have always sought elusive answers to simple questions: What living things exist? Where do they exist? And are they related? Under conditions of climate change, growing environmental threat, and mass extinction, Farrington says, researchers are asking urgent new questions: Can species adapt to climate change? Where will they move? And how can we improve their chances for survival? This may be the first generation of researchers with the tools to discover the answers; with luck and new scientific knowledge, it will not be the last generation with the chance to try.

The building's superclear glass permits transparent views through the Academy from outside the south entry.

CALIFORNIA ACADEMY OF SCIENCES MUSEUM DIRECTORS

(Note: From 1868 until 1914 the director of the museum was an elected officer. Elections were held each January at the annual meeting.)

1853—1867	No director, curators only.
1868	Robert E. C. Stearns (January 13-May 4; resigned because he was leaving the state)
1869—1874	Hiram G. Bloomer (January 4, 1869-September 1874; died while in office)
1875—1876	Albert Kellogg (January 4, 1875-January 2, 1876)
1876—1887	William G. W. Harford (January 3, 1876-January 2, 1887)
1887—1892	James Graham Cooper (January 3, 1887-January 3, 1892)
1892—1896	Jacob Z. Davis (January 4, 1892-October 1896; died while in office)
1897—1902	Charles A. Keeler (January 4, 1897-January 5, 1902)
1902—1913	Leverett Mills Loomis (January 6, 1902-January 5, 1913)
1913—1914	Guilian P. Rixford (January 6, 1913-March 14, 1914)
1914—1932	Barton Warren Evermann (March 15, 1914-September 27, 1932; hospitalized June 21, granted leave beginning September 1, died September 27)
1932—1934	(Acting Director) Carl Ewald Grunsky (September 1, 1932-June 9, 1934; died while in office)
1934—1938	(Acting Director) Frank Mace MacFarland (June 18, 1934-1938)
1938—1963	Robert C. Miller (September 1, 1938-September 30, 1963)
1963—1982	George E. Lindsay (October 1, 1963-February 28, 1982)
1982—1988	Frank H. Talbot (March 1, 1982-December 1988)
1989	(Acting Director) John McCosker (January-May 14, 1989)
1989—1994	Roy Eisenhardt (May 15, 1989-May 15, 1994)
1994	(Acting Director) John McCosker (May 16, 1994-September 30, 1994)
1994—1997	Evelyn Handler (October 1, 1994-1997)
1997—2007	J. Patrick Kociolek (Interim Executive Director: October 24, 1997-February 12, 1998; Executive Director: 1998-2007)
2007—PRESENT	Gregory C. Farrington

CALIFORNIA ACADEMY OF SCIENCES PRESIDENTS

THE EVOLUTION OF THE PRESIDENCY:

1853—1870:   The Academy president is elected by the entire membership, heads the organization, and presides at all Academy meetings.

1871—1952:   Two groups of officers: the Board of Trustees (business affairs) and the Council (scientific and educational matters). The president is elected by the entire membership, presides over Academy meetings, and heads the Council.

1952—1959:   Corporate membership (mainly Fellows) elects the Board of Trustees and the Council. The president is elected from within the Council.

1959—PRESENT: The president is elected from within the Board of Trustees, and must be a scientist. The Nominating Committee presents a slate of recommended officer candidates, and unless the Fellows nominate opposing candidates, the recommendations are unanimously adopted by the Board of Trustees. The president presides over the Science Council, which advises the Board of Trustees.

1853—1856	Andrew Randall (May 23, 1853–January 6, 1856)	1912—1934	C. E. Grunsky (January 2, 1912–June 9, 1934; died while in office)
1856—1867	Leander Ransom (January 7, 1856–January 6, 1867)		
1867—1868	Josiah D. Whitney (January 7, 1867–April 20, 1868; resigned because he was leaving the state)	1934—1946	Frank Mace MacFarland (June 18, 1934-1946)
		1946—1950	Maurice E. Lombardi (1946–February 1950)
1868—1872	James Blake (May 4, 1868–January 1, 1872)	1950—1953	Francis P. Farquhar (February 1950-1953)
1872—1887	George Davidson (January 2, 1872–January 16, 1887)	1953—1954	E. B. Babcock (October 1953-1954)
		1954—1959	Ira L. Wiggins (1954–October 18, 1959)
1887—1896	Harvey W. Harkness (January 17, 1887–January 19, 1896)	1959—1966	A. Starker Leopold (October 19, 1959-1966)
1896—1898	David Starr Jordan (January 20, 1896–January 16, 1898)	1966—1968	J. Wyatt Durham (1966–October 20, 1968)
		1968—1971	A. Starker Leopold (October 21, 1968–October 1971)
1898—1900	William E. Ritter (January 17, 1898–January 14, 1900)	1971—1975	Ian Campbell (October 1971–October 1975)
		1975—1978	Lincoln Constance (October 1975–October 1978)
1900—1903	David Starr Jordan (January 15, 1900–January 18, 1903)	1978—1981	Richard H. Jahns (October 1978–October 1981)
		1981—1982	F. Clark Howell (October 1981–October 19, 1982)
1903—1904	William Alvord (January 19, 1903–December 21, 1904; died while in office)	1982—1985	Bruce A. Bolt (October 20, 1982–October 15, 1985)
1905—1909	Eusebius J. Molera (January 3, 1905–January 3, 1909)	1985—1993	James C. Kelley (October 16, 1985–April 29, 1993)
		1993—1997	William A. Clemens (April 30, 1993-1997)
1909—1912	David Starr Jordan (January 4, 1909–January 1, 1912)	1997—2003	John S. Pearse (1997-2003)
		2003—PRESENT	Ward B. Watt

PRINCIPAL PHOTOGRAPHERS

MICHAEL DENANCE

TIM GRIFFITH

DONG LIN

plus

ROLLO BECK

GERRY AND BUFF CORSI

CHARLOTTE FIORITO

MARGARET HANNA

KANG KIANG

CAROLINE KOPP

DAVID LIITTSCHWAGER

MAYA LIN

JOHN MCCOSKER

JON MCNEAL

HOPE MENG

SUSAN MIDDLETON

ELMER MOSS

BRETT TERPELUK

LLOYD ULLBERG

CINTHIA WEN

ACKNOWLEDGMENTS

from Greg Farrington I want to recognize five individuals who led the creation of this wonderful book. Don Skeoch, who accepted the challenge of overseeing the project and making this book a reality. Jean Farrington, who spent time organizing material and ensuring that the book is the worthy repository that it is. Rhonda Rubinstein, who applied her extensive experience in publishing and creative fields to the challenge of making this beautiful volume such a success. Karren Elsbernd, for researching and collecting photographs from the Academy's archives. Finally, this book would not exist without the commitment and dedication that Alison Brown brought to the project—and to the Academy—during the last decade. Our new global institution owes a great deal to her talent and dedication.

from Susan Wels In preparing the text for this book, I spoke to Academy staff, architects, designers, builders, and horticulturalists who were uniformly enthusiastic and cooperative. I am grateful for the assistance of Frank Almeda, Barbara Andrews, Chris Andrews, Richard Bingham, Alison Brown, Meg Burke, Shawn Byers, Gordon Chang, Cameron Cooper, Jack Dumbacher, Brian Fisher, Randi Fisher, Terry Gosliner, Kang Kiang, Healy Hamilton, Russell Hartman, Tom Hennes, Jonathan Katz, Pat Kilduff, Patrick Kociolek, Martha Kropf, Nancy Losey, John McCosker, Michelle McClellan, Jon McNeal, Scott Moran, Olaf de Nooyer, Bill Patterson, Mike Shakespear, Bart Shepherd, Stephanie Stone, Carol Tang, Bill Wilson, and Ryan Wyatt.

from John E. McCosker I particularly thank Pam McCosker and Keith Howell for their help and advice, as well as Frank Almeda, Foster Bam, Joe Brennan, Steve Craig, Larry Currie, Roy Eisenhardt, Karren Elsbernd, Phyllis Ensrud, Bill Eschmeyer, Terry Gosliner, Paul Humann, Patrick Kociolek, Gary Larson, Alan Leviton, Dong Lin, George Lindsay, R. C. Miller, Bing Quock, Walter Schneebeli, Tom Tucker, and Michele Wellck.

FURTHER READING

To learn more about the rich and colorful history of the California Academy of Sciences, please see the following resources: Theodore Henry Hittell's *The California Academy of Sciences, A Narrative History, 1853–1906,* edited by A. E. Leviton and M. L. Aldrich (San Francisco: California Academy of Sciences, 1997); *The History of Steinhart Aquarium: A Very Fishy Tale,* by John E. McCosker (Virginia Beach, Va.: The Donning Company, 1998); and many articles in the Academy's award-winning magazines *Pacific Discovery* and *California Wild.*